W9-BSQ-035

LEARNING THE ARTLESS ART

As a result of years of disciplined study, Joe Hyams explains how mastering a martial art can foster a student's personal and spiritual growth:

> "A *dojo* [practice hall] is a miniature cosmos where we make contact with ourselves—our fears, anxieties, reactions, and habits. It is an arena of confined conflict where we confront an opponent who is not an opponent but rather a partner engaged in helping us understand ourselves more fully. . . ."

Technical knowledge alone is not enough. A martial artist must simultaneously transcend technique *and* develop intuitive action so that the art becomes an artless art, a way to physical excellence, a way to spiritual enlightenment.

Bantam Books of Related Interest
Ask your bookseller for the books you have missed

BRUCE TEGNER'S COMPLETE BOOK OF KARATE
    by Bruce Tegner

THE DANCING WU LI MASTERS by Gary Zukav

GRIST FOR THE MILL by Ram Dass

HOW TO MEDITATE: A GUIDE TO SELF-DISCOVERY
    by Lawrence LeShan

IF YOU MEET THE BUDDHA ON THE ROAD, KILL HIM!
    Sheldon Kopp

JOURNEY OF AWAKENING by Ram Dass

THE LAZY MAN'S GUIDE TO ENLIGHTENMENT
    by Thaddeus Golas

PASSAGES by Gail Sheehy

THE TAO OF PHYSICS by Fritjof Capra

ZEN AND THE ART OF MOTORCYCLE MAINTENANCE
    by Robert M. Pirsig

ZEN
IN
THE
MARTIAL
ARTS

JOE HYAMS

Photographs by
Kenneth McGowan & Doug Coder

BANTAM BOOKS
TORONTO · NEW YORK · LONDON · SYDNEY

*To Pat Strong, who patiently and
wisely guided me in each stage of my martial arts
training for many years and always provided an example
of the complete martial artist.*

*And to my wife, Elke, who has never
entirely understood my absorption with the arts but,
nevertheless, has always been encouraging.*

*This low-priced Bantam Book
has been completely reset in a type face
designed for easy reading, and was printed
from new plates. It contains the complete
text of the original hard-cover edition.*
NOT ONE WORD HAS BEEN OMITTED.

ZEN IN THE MARTIAL ARTS
A Bantam Book

PRINTING HISTORY
Tarcher edition published October 1979
Bantam edition / July 1982

All rights reserved.
Copyright © 1979 by Joe Hyams.
Cover art courtesy of J. P. Tarcher / St. Martin's Press
*This book may not be reproduced in whole or in part, by
mimeograph or any other means, without permission.
For information address: Bantam Books, Inc.*

ISBN 0-553-22510-3

Published simultaneously in the United States and Canada

Bantam Books are published by Bantam Books, Inc. Its trademark, consisting of the words ''Bantam Books'' and the por-
trayal of a rooster, is Registered in U.S. Patent and Trademark
Office and in other countries. Marca Registrada. Bantam
Books, Inc., 666 Fifth Avenue, New York, New York 10103.

PRINTED IN THE UNITED STATES OF AMERICA

0 9 8 7 6 5 4

CONTENTS

ACKNOWLEDGMENTS

*I*n the text of this book I have introduced most of the masters with whom I studied during the past two and a half decades. But I would be remiss if I did not give special thanks to the following: George Waite, for his advice, special training, and friendship; Bob Phillips, who, although not a martial artist, has the spirit, fighting ability, and good sportsmanship typical of all professional athletes; Bernie Bernheim, who, starting to study karate at the age of fifty-seven and becoming a black belt at sixty-one, is an inspiration for all who believe martial arts are only for the physically young; Emile Farkas, for his advice and comments on the text; Stan Schmidt of Johannesburg, who in the heart of South Africa runs a traditional dojo which has produced many world champions; and Larry Tatum, who has graciously allowed me to train from time to time with his classes at Ed Parker's dojo in Santa Monica, California.

ZEN
IN THE
MARTIAL
ARTS

*S*everal hundred books have been written about performing the Oriental martial arts, but no more than a handful address the significance of Zen in the martial arts. This is an unfortunate oversight since the martial arts in their finest form are much more than a physical contest between two opponents—a means of imposing one's will or inflicting damage upon another. Rather, for the true master, karate, kung-fu, aikido, wing-chun, and all the other martial arts are essentially avenues through which they can achieve spiritual serenity, mental tranquility, and the deepest self-confidence.

Yet I had studied the martial arts for several years before becoming aware of this. In the early stages of training, like most students, I spent my time learning and refining complex physical techniques and movements. Only occasionally did a *sifu* ("instructor" in Chinese) hint that there were other lessons to be mastered.

Of course, it was not my intention when I started studying karate in 1952 to become involved with Zen or any other spiritual discipline. In fact, nothing could have been further from my mind. Had anyone told me where my path would eventually lead, I would probably have dismissed the notion as nonsense, because I associated Zen with mysticism and prided myself in being a pragmatist. Only after several years of training did I come to realize that the deepest purpose of the martial arts is to serve as a vehicle for personal spiritual development.

The martial arts began to develop this emphasis on personal spiritual growth in the sixteenth century, when the need for fighting skills in the Orient diminished. The martial arts were transformed from a practical means of combat-to-the-death to spiritual educational training that emphasized the personal development of the participant. Thus the art of fighting with the sword, *kenjutsu*, became transformed into "the way of the sword," *kendo*. Soon other martial arts were given the ending - *do*, which means "the way," or more fully, "the way to enlightenment, self-realization, and understanding." This Zen element is reflected to various degrees in aikido, judo, karate-do, tae-kwon-do, hapkido, and jeet-kune-do, among others.

The role of Zen in the martial arts defies easy definition because Zen has no theory; it is an inner knowing for which there is no clearly stated dogma. The Zen of martial arts deemphasizes the power of the intellect and extols that of intuitive action. Its ultimate aim is to free the individual from anger, illusion, and false passion.

It is possible for the student to make contact with Zen in the martial arts only by a slow and roundabout route. Once I came to this realization, familiar to all true masters of the arts, I began to keep notes on my discoveries. For the past decade, *Zen in the Martial Arts* has been the great story over my horizon, the book I most wanted to write. But there was always another master to study with or another discipline to learn before I felt I was prepared.

This is not a book, however, for the reader who wishes to master Zen, for the concepts central to that tradition are certainly not acquired from the written word. Nor is this a book for those who expect to learn how to perform the amazing feats of martial artists who break boards and bricks with their bare hands and easily defeat several opponents at a time. The reader interested only in learning about the physical aspects of the martial arts can adventure alone in the literature without my guidance. Instead, this is a book from which readers may learn to apply the principles of Zen, as reflected in the martial arts, to their lives and thus open up a potential source of inner strength they may never have dreamt they possessed.

My own involvement with the martial arts began in 1952, when I was a Hollywood columnist for the *New York Herald Tribune.* I was sedentary, overweight, restless, easily bored, and constantly seeking new adventures. I had no clear awareness of who I was or where my life or my career was going. To make matters worse I was anxious, intimidated by authority, insecure, and hostile to compensate for my insecurity. Every day I interviewed film stars, many of whom were younger than I. Because I often resented their success, my interview technique was to needle them until they responded with something quotable.

One day Bronislaw Kaper, the Academy-Award winning film composer, recognized my technique for exactly what it was and suggested I study karate. "The exercise might help you slim down and allow you to work off some of your hostilities," he suggested. At that time karate was new on the Hollywood scene and was viewed merely as an exotic Asian way of fighting. Such concepts as consciousness raising, taking control of one's life, and heightened self-awareness were as yet unheard of. Only recently have we come to understand the relationship between sports and personal or spiritual growth.

When Kaper arranged for my first lesson with karate master Ed Parker, I accepted with the thought that even

3

if I learned nothing I would still gather enough material for several newspaper columns since a handful of stars, including Elvis Presley, were then studying with Parker.

In those days Parker was teaching kenpo-karate, an American form of Chinese boxing, in the weight room of a Beverly Hills health club. At our first meeting he told me, "I am not going to *show* you my art. I am going to *share* it with you. If I *show* it to you it becomes an exhibition, and in time it will be pushed so far into the back of your mind that it will be lost. But by *sharing* it with you, you will not only retain it forever, but I, too, will improve."

I soon learned that the concept of the *teacher* learning from the lesson is basic to all good martial arts instruction. For this reason perhaps the practice hall—*dojo* (Japanese), *dojang* (Korean), *kwoon* (Chinese)—where martial arts is studied is traditionally called "The Place of Enlightenment."

A dojo is a miniature cosmos where we make contact with ourselves—our fears, anxieties, reactions, and habits. It is an arena of confined conflict where we confront an opponent who is not an opponent but rather a partner engaged in helping us understand ourselves more fully. It is a place where we can learn a great deal in a short time about who we are and how we react in the world. The conflicts that take place inside the dojo help us handle conflicts that take place outside. The total concentration and discipline required to study martial arts carries over to daily life. The activity in the dojo calls on us to constantly attempt new things, so it is also a source of learning—in Zen terminology, a source of self-enlightenment.

There is a Buddhist saying that anyplace can be a dojo. I have studied shodokan karate in a beautiful modern building in Johannesburg, South Africa; judo in the back room of a Japanese restaurant in London, England; jujitsu in a *sport halle* in Munich, Germany. But most of my study in hapkido, aikido, tae-kwon-do and wing-chun has been in Los Angeles where stores are frequently converted into martial arts studios. Bruce Lee taught jeet-kune-do to screenwriter Stirling Silliphant and me in the driveway of my home.

Each dojo is presided over by a sifu, or *sensei* (Japanese), meaning "master." *Sen* means "before," and *sei* means "born." The literal meaning of the Japanese word is "one who is born before"; thus, the one who is born before you is your teacher. This refers less to chronological age (some of my teachers have been young enough to be my children) than to the teacher's wisdom: In spiritual terms he or she is my elder, and thus my teacher.

The martial arts sensei is very much like the Zen master; he has not sought out the student, nor does he prevent him from leaving. If the student wants guidance in climbing the steep path to expertise, the instructor is willing to act as guide—on the condition that the student be prepared to take care of himself along the way. The instructor's function is to delegate to the student exactly those tasks which he is capable of mastering, and then to leave him as much as possible to himself and his inner abilities. The student may follow in the footsteps of his guide or choose an alternate path—the choice is his.

The instructor first teaches technique *(waza)* without discussing its significance; he simply waits for the student to discover this for himself. If the student has the necessary dedication, and the teacher provides the proper spiritual inspiration, then the meaning and essence of the martial arts will finally reveal themselves to him.

Although one can read about the Zen in the martial arts, true knowledge of it is experiential. How do we explain the taste of sugar? Verbal descriptions do not give us the sensation. To know the taste, one must experience it. The philosophy of the arts is not meant to be mused over and intellectualized; it is meant to be experienced. Thus, inevitably, words will convey only part of the meaning.

In more than twenty years of studying the martial arts I have not retired to a Zen monastery nor retreated from the pressures of working and living in a competitive society. But I have found that when I attain the spiritual goals of the martial arts, the quality of my life has been dramatically altered—enriching my relationships with people, as well as keeping me in closer touch with myself. I have come to see that enlightenment simply means recognizing the inherent harmony of ordinary life.

I put this book forward to you, then, in the spirit of sharing what I have learned, and in the hope that some may wish to travel a similar path. Perhaps by sharing my experiences I will also learn more, because that, too, is the way of Zen.

A man who has attained mastery
of an art reveals it in his every action.
—SAMURAI MAXIM

Knowing others is wisdom, knowing yourself is Enlightenment.
—LAO-TZU

EMPTY
YOUR
CUP

*T*he air was muggy and fetid in the Long Beach Sports Arena on that summer day in 1964. The air conditioning was malfunctioning and the crowd at the International Karate Tournament was getting restless after watching hours of matches. Then Ed Parker, sponsor of the annual event, took the microphone and introduced Bruce Lee, who was to put on a demonstration of jeet-kune-do. There was an instant hush and all heads craned forward. Before his movie career began Bruce Lee was already a legend among martial artists.

Bruce walked onto the elevated boxing ring wearing a simple, black, tailor-made kung-fu uniform. He spoke quietly for a few moments about his art and then began the demonstration. It is always impressive to watch a large, muscular man perform karate, overwhelming the observer with a display of sheer, vibrant power. But to me, it is even more impressive to see a slightly built man executing techniques with blinding speed, his motions as quick and elegant as those of a bird in flight. When

9

Bruce finished there was a moment of silence and then shattering applause.

Some weeks later a friend arranged for me to meet Bruce, from whom I hoped to take private lessons. Bruce was highly selective about the students he chose to teach, and this meeting was to be a kind of audition for me.

Since he gave only private lessons and had no formal studio, the meeting was at my home. He arrived promptly and I went out into the front yard to meet him. At first glance he appeared even smaller than he looked on stage. He was wearing snug-fitting, full-length athletic pants and a green tank top shirt that revealed rippling muscles. He was smiling when we shook hands, but he quickly got to the point.

"Why do you want to study with me?" he asked.

"Because I was impressed with your demonstration and because I've heard you are the best."

"You've studied other martial arts?" he asked.

"For a long time," I answered, "but I stopped some time ago and now I want to start over again."

Bruce nodded and asked me to demonstrate some of the techniques I already knew. We went out to my driveway and he watched intently as I went through the various *katas,* or exercises, from other disciplines. Then he asked me to execute some basic kicks, blocks, and punches on a bag hanging from a rafter of the garage.

"Do you realize you will have to unlearn all you have learned and start over again?" he asked.

"No," I said.

Bruce smiled and placed his hand lightly on my shoulder. "Let me tell you a story my sifu told me," he said. "It is about the Japanese Zen master who received a university professor who came to inquire about Zen.

"It was obvious to the master from the start of the conversation that the professor was not so much interested in learning about Zen as he was in impressing the master with his own opinions and knowledge. The master listened patiently and finally suggested they have

10

tea. The master poured his visitor's cup full and then kept on pouring.

"The professor watched the cup overflowing until he could no longer restrain himself. 'The cup is overfull, no more will go in.'

" 'Like this cup,' the master said, 'you are full of your own opinions and speculations. How can I show you Zen unless you first empty your cup?' "

Bruce studied my face. "You understand the point?"

"Yes," I said. "You want me to empty my mind of past knowledge and old habits so that I will be open to new learning."

"Precisely," said Bruce. "And now we are ready to begin your first lesson."

This does not mean that Bruce prevented me from applying a critical mind to his teaching. In fact, he welcomed discussion, even argument. But when challenged too long on a point his reply was always, "At least empty your cup and try."

Later I learned that Bruce practiced what he taught. As a youth in Hong Kong he had studied *wing-chun,* a branch of kung-fu, under the celebrated master, Yip Man. When he came to America as a teenager he observed Ed Parker's kenpo-karate, taking from it many hand techniques that appealed to him. From tae-kwon-do he borrowed the devastating kicks that make the Korean style so formidable. He also studied other styles of martial arts, taking from all of them whatever he thought useful. Although considered one of the best martial artists of his time, he was always learning, always in a constant process of change and improvement. He truly kept his cup empty.

Bruce had not only developed his physical abilities to a point of perfection, he had also honed his mind with the study of Zen. His den in Los Angeles was stacked ceiling-high with worn volumes of the Zen masters written in Chinese and in English.

It has been more than a decade since my first lesson with Bruce, and I am now in my mid-fifties. With half a century of life experience behind me, I sometimes get impatient with a new idea or technique. But when I feel impatient or act dogmatically self-assured, I remind myself of the lesson Bruce taught me, and I try to empty my cup to make room for new methods and ideas.

That was my first real lesson in Zen in the martial arts and its application to life—although at the time I didn't recognize it as Zen. It was merely good sense—which is what Zen really is.

Nothing is impossible to a willing mind.
—BOOKS OF HAN DYNASTY

When you seek it, you cannot find it.
—ZEN RIDDLE

14

PROCESS
NOT
PRODUCT

Master Bong Soo Han is a Korean of medium height with a full head of iron-gray hair. There is quiet authority in everything he says and does. No movement or word is superfluous. He is the traditional martial artist who learned hapkido from his master in Korea who, in turn, learned it from a master who had been taught by a long, continuous line of other masters. A session with Master Han is not just a workout, it is also a lesson in life. I always feel enriched after leaving his dojang.

I was fifty years old when I started the study of hapkido with Master Han. From the beginning the learning process was slow and often difficult for me because hapkido requires an extremely limber body. My body had stiffened with age and I had back problems that threw me off balance and made every kick above waist level painful. My learning was further complicated by the presence of much younger men who were able to do easily that which required tremendous effort and concentration on my part. There were many times when I considered quitting, a fact Master Han recognized.

One afternoon following a workout, Master Han invited me to have tea with him. After he had served the tea, he began, "You will never learn to do any endeavor properly unless you are willing to give yourself time. I think you are accustomed to having everything come easily to you, but this is not the way of life or of the martial arts."

"I am patient," I said.

"We are not talking now about patience," he answered. "To be patient is to have the capacity of calm endurance. To give yourself time is to actively work toward a goal without setting a limit on how long you will work."

He had touched the core of my problem. I had given myself a set amount of time to become reasonably proficient in his style, and I was frustrating myself because I didn't seem to be achieving the goal quickly enough. When I eliminated the deadline from my mind it was like removing a weight from my body. Within a few months I was able to perform with the rest of the class.

Equally important, I used Master Han's advice to resolve an immediate problem. I was working on a book at that time, and the writing was going slowly. That frustrated me because I had agreed to start another project in short order and it was weighing on my mind. Now I could see that my focus was wrong. I was doing the same thing I had done with hapkido. I should have been concerned with the *process* of working on the book rather than on its completion. Once I removed the time constraint from my mind and approached the book without an arbitrary limit, I was able to dedicate myself to the writing and work without anxiety.

For the uncontrolled there is no wisdom,
nor for the uncontrolled is there the power of
concentration; and for him without concentration
there is no peace. And for the unpeaceful,
how can there be happiness?
—BHAGAVAD GITA

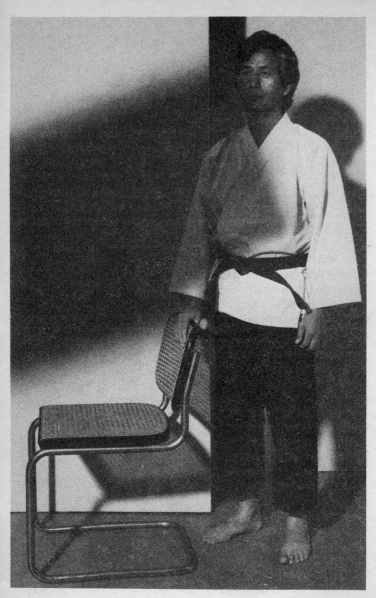

SEIZE
THE
MOMENT

*O*ne day while working out at Master Han's dojang, I was going through the hapkido motions mechanically, doing things poorly that I knew how to do well, and constantly glancing at the clock.

"Your mind is elsewhere," Master Han said after a few minutes.

I admitted that in truth my mind was elsewhere; I had barely managed to sandwich in my lesson between appointments.

Master Han bowed to me, signifying the lesson was ended.

After I had dressed and was on my way out of the dojang, I found him at the doorway waiting for me.

"You must learn to live in the present," he said. "Not in the future or the past. Zen teaches that life must be seized at the moment. By living in the present you are in full contact with yourself and your environment, your energy is not dissipated and is always available. In the present there are no regrets as there are in the past. By thinking of the future, you dilute the present. The time to live is now.

"As long as what you are doing at the moment is *exactly* what you are doing at that moment and nothing else, you are one with yourself and with what you are doing—and that is Zen; while doing something you are doing it at the fullest."

I reflected on what Master Han had said. One of the major reasons I like martial arts is that it demands total concentration. For a few hours each week I can block out all the problems and pressures of my daily life. The speed with which a martial arts practice session or bout takes place allows no break between "points" or time for reflection.

But on that day I had allowed myself to be distracted. My thoughts were split between the meeting I had just concluded and the one that was about to take place. My mind had not been on the activity of the moment.

I realized how often while working I allowed my mind to wander thus, dissipating both energy and concentration. I resolved that I would train myself not to let that happen. I would give each activity my fullest concentration. When I returned to my office, I wrote on a small filing card, "Seize life at the moment," and thumbtacked it over my desk.

The card is still tacked above my desk, and I reread it each time I find myself distracted. Since that day I have continually reminded myself to focus on the moment, rather than allowing my mind to wander to past or future.

Patience, the essential quality of a man.
—KWAI-KOO-TSU

CONQUER HASTE

I was having tea with Master Han in his office when the mailman arrived with a letter from the master's family in Korea.

Knowing he had been eagerly anticipating the letter, I paused in our conversation, expecting him to tear open the envelope and hastily scan the contents. Instead, he put the letter aside, turned to me, and continued our conversation.

The following day I remarked on his self-control, saying that I would have read the letter at once.

"I did what I would have done had I been alone," he said. "I put the letter aside until I had conquered haste. Then when I set my hand to it, I opened it as though it were something precious."

I puzzled over this comment a moment, knowing he meant it to be a lesson for me. Finally I said I didn't understand what such patience led to.

"It leads to this," he said. "Those who are patient in the trivial things in life and control themselves will one day have the same mastery in great and important things."

KNOW
YOUR
LIMITS

*B*ruce Lee and I were having *dim sum,* a traditional Chinese breakfast of meat-filled pastries, in a downtown Los Angeles restaurant after a lesson. I seized on this opportunity to tell him that I was discouraged. At forty-five, I felt I was too old and my body too stiff to achieve any real ability in jeet-kune-do.

"You will never learn anything new unless you are ready to accept yourself *with* your limitations," Bruce answered. "You must accept the fact that you are capable, in some directions and limited in others, and you must develop your capabilities."

"But ten years ago I could easily kick over my head," I said. "Now I need half an hour to limber up before I can do it."

Bruce set his chopsticks down alongside his plate, clasped his hands lightly on his lap, and smiled at me. "That was ten years ago," he said gently. "So you are older today and your body has changed. Everyone has physical limitations to overcome."

"That's all very well for you to say," I replied. "If ever

a man was born with natural ability as a martial artist, it is you."

Bruce laughed. "I'm going to tell you something very few people know. I became a martial artist *in spite of* my limitations."

I was shocked. In my view, Bruce was a perfect physical specimen and I said so.

"You probably are not aware of it," he said, "but my right leg is almost one inch shorter than the left. That fact dictated the best stance for me—my left foot leading. Then I found that because the right leg was shorter, I had an advantage with certain types of kicks,

since the uneven stomp gave me greater impetus.

"And I wear contact lenses. Since childhood I have been near-sighted, which meant that when I wasn't wearing glasses, I had difficulty seeing an opponent when he wasn't up close. I originally started to study wing-chun because it is an ideal technique for close-in fighting.

"I accepted my limitations for what they were and capitalized on them. And that's what *you* must learn to do. You say you are unable to kick over your head without a long warm-up, but the real question is, is it really necessary to kick that high? The fact is that until

27

recently, martial artists rarely kicked above knee height. Head-high kicks are mostly for show. So perfect your kicks at waist level and they will be so formidable you'll never need to kick higher.

"Instead of trying to do everything well, do those things perfectly of which you are capable. Although most expert martial artists have spent years mastering hundreds of techniques and movements, in a bout, or *kumite,* a champion may actually use only four or five techniques over and over again. These are the techniques which he has perfected and which he knows he can depend on."

I protested. "But the fact still remains that my real competition is the advancing years."

"Stop comparing yourself at forty-five with the man you were at twenty or thirty," Bruce answered. "The past is an illusion. You must learn to live in the present and accept yourself for what you are *now.* What you lack in flexibility and agility you must make up with knowledge and constant practice."

For the next few months, instead of spending time trying to get limber enough to kick over my head, I worked on my waist-high kicks until they satisfied even Bruce.

Then one day late in 1965, he came by my house to say goodbye before leaving for Hong Kong where, he said, he intended to become the biggest star in films. "You remember our talk about limitations?" he asked. "Well, I'm limited by my size and difficulty in English and the fact that I'm Chinese, and there never has been a big Chinese star in American films. But I have spent the last three years studying movies, and I think the time is ripe for a good martial arts film—and I am the best qualified to star in it. *My capabilities exceed my limitations.*"

Bruce's capabilities did in fact exceed his limitations and, until his youthful death, he was one of the biggest stars in films. His career was a perfect illustration of his teaching: As we discover and improve our strong points, they come to outweigh our weaknesses.

Power of mind is infinite while
brawn is limited.
—KOICHI TOHEI

EVEN
THE MASTERS
HAVE
MASTERS

The beginning student in most martial arts disciplines wears a white belt that, according to tradition, signifies innocence. With the passage of time the belt becomes soiled from handling and use, so the second stage of learning is signified by a brown belt. As more time passes the belt becomes darker until it is black—the black belt stage. With even more use the black belt becomes frayed, almost white, signifying that the wearer is returning again to innocence—a Zen characteristic of human perfection.

Many martial arts systems have various colors of belts between white and born as well as degrees of brown and black, a constant reminder to the student that there is more to learn beyond whatever proficiency he or she may already have. This awareness extends even to the masters, each of whom had a master before him.

Ed Parker, for example, considers himself a novice compared with William Chow, his master in Hawaii;

Master Bong Soo Han speaks with reverence about the ability of his master in Korea, Yong Sul Choi; Bruce Lee always spoke with awe of his master in Hong Kong, Yip Man, who was also Jim Lau's sifu; Stan Schmidt of South Africa travels halfway around the world to Los Angeles once a year to study with his master, Nishyama; while Camilla Fluxman of Los Angeles returns home to South Africa whenever she can to study again with her master, Stan Schmidt. This endless circle of student and master gives both the teacher and the taught the feeling of being part of a continuum of learning.

My own learning experience in the martial arts has always been like a staircase with countless landings. With each step upward the goal—spiritual and physical unification of mind and body—seems nearer. But there are always landings, or plateaus, at which learning seems to stop and the staircase winds infinitely upward. At such times I have often felt frustrated and discouraged. I have mentioned this experience to martial-arts friends, and each admits that he, too, reaches such a plateau from time to time. The experience is common to us all.

George Waite, my good friend and mentor, recalled his brown belt days in karate and how discouraged he became when he saw someone far better than he, although he considered himself good.

"When that happened," he said, "I used to go into the dojo and watch the white belts. I saw that, compared with them, I was good. But then I'd watch the black belts and become inspired all over again, seeing how much better it was possible to become. When I finally became a black belt I realized that I really knew nothing compared with my sifu, and I was discouraged until he told me how great was his master."

Despite my many years of martial arts study, I recognize how little I really know compared with true masters of the arts. Only by constantly exposing myself to someone better than I have I been able to improve. It is inspiring to know that even the masters have masters, and that we are all learners.

King Hsuan of Chou heard of Po Kung-i, who was reputed to be the strongest man in his kingdom. The King was dismayed when they met, since Po looked so weak. When the King asked Po how strong he was, Po said mildly, "I can break the leg of a spring grasshopper and withstand the winds of an autumn cicada." Aghast, the King thundered, "I can tear rhinocerous leather and drag nine buffaloes by the tail, yet I am shamed by my weakness. How can you be famous?" Po smiled and answered quietly, "My teacher was Tzu Shang-chi'ui, whose strength was without peer in the world, but even his relatives never knew it because *he never used it.*"
—ANONYMOUS

LENGTHEN
YOUR
LINE

I first met with kenpo-karate master Ed Parker in 1952 in a Beverly Hills gym where he rented space. A handsome, six-foot-tall Hawaiian with a thick thatch of black hair, Parker reminded me of a huge tree, with arms like powerful boughs and bare feet rooted firmly on the canvas mat. (Despite his size, he is a whirlwind in motion.) He was wearing an old, loose-fitting gi, a two-piece cotton uniform worn by most martial artists. The gi, like his black belt, was white in places from fraying and repeated launderings. His face was serene and peaceful, as though he had just completed meditating.

I well remember one of my initial sessions at his dojo in Los Angeles where I was practicing *kumite* (sparring) with a more skillful opponent. To make up for my lack of knowledge and experience, I tried deceptive, tricky moves that were readily countered. I was outclassed, and Parker watched me get roundly trounced. When the match was over I was dejected. Parker invited me into his office, a small, sparsely furnished room with only a scarred desk and battered chairs.

"Why are you so upset?" he asked.

"Because I couldn't score."

Parker got up from behind the desk and with a piece of chalk drew a line on the floor about five feet long. "How can you make this line shorter?" he asked.

I studied the line and gave him several answers, including cutting the line in many pieces.

He shook his head and drew a second line, longer than the first. "Now how does the first line look?"

"Shorter," I said.

Parker nodded. "It is always better to improve and strengthen your own line or knowledge than to try and cut your opponent's line." He accompanied me to the door and added, "Think about what I have just said."

I did think about it and studied hard for the next several months, developing greater skills, increasing my knowledge and ability. The next time I went on the mat with the same opponent he, too, had improved. But I fared far better than I had previously because I had raised my level of knowledge as well as developing my skills.

Not long after, I realized I could apply the principle Parker had taught me to my tennis game. An avid weekend tennis player, I frequently found myself pitted against better players, and when things started to go badly for me on the court I often resorted to trickery—slicing the ball, trying to hit it with a spin, attempting difficult drop shots. Invariably I lost and was frustrated. Instead of trying to better my game I was trying to "cut their line." I recognized that I had to play to my best ability rather than try to worsen my opponent's play. Keeping Parker's advice in mind, my game soon improved.

It has been nearly three decades since then, and in the intervening years Parker has taught his art to thousands of students. Even long after their training they think of him as a good friend—and as a wise and gentle sifu who embodies the martial arts' spirit and philosophy.

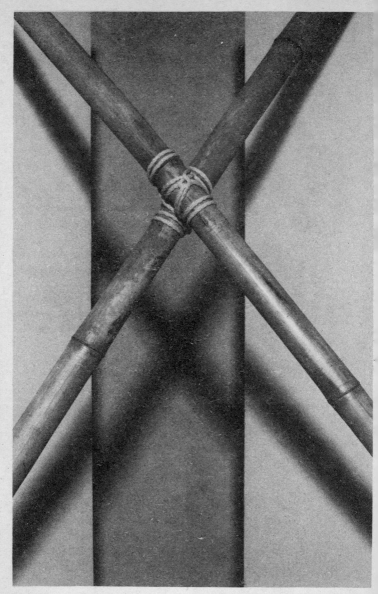

DO
NOT
DISTURB

Many of my jeet-kune-do lessons with Bruce Lee were shared with Stirling Silliphant, one of the most successful screenwriters in America. Often, after lessons, the three of us would retire to my backyard and, over a glass of fruit juice, sit and talk. These few moments were precious to me because, invariably, I gained an insight into one or both of my friends.

On one such occasion, we talked about the difference between wasting time and spending time. Bruce was the first to speak.

"To spend time is to pass it in a specified manner," he said. "We are spending it during lessons just as we are spending it now in conversation. To waste time is to expend it thoughtlessly or carelessly. We all have time to either spend or waste and it is our decision what to do with it. But once passed, it is gone forever."

"It's the most precious commodity we have," agreed Sterling. "I always view my time as divided into infinite moments or transactions or contacts. Anyone who steals my time is stealing my life because they are taking my existence from me. As I get older, I realize that time is the only thing I have left. So when someone comes to me with a project, I estimate the time it will take me to do it and then I ask myself, 'Do I want to spend weeks or months of what little time I have on this project? Is it worth it or am I just wasting my time?' If I consider the project time-worthy I do it.

"I apply the same yardstick to social relations. I will not permit people to steal my time. I have limited my friends to those people with whom time passes happily. There are moments in my life—necessary moments— when I don't do anything but what is my choice. The choice of how I spend my time is mine, and it is not dictated by social convention."

After Stirling finished talking, Bruce looked out into space for a few moments. When he finally spoke, it was to ask if he could make a telephone call.

When he came back, Bruce was smiling. "I just cancelled an appointment," he said. "It was with someone who wanted to waste my time and not help me spend it."

As he left us, Bruce turned to Stirling and said, "Today you were the teacher. I realized for the first time how much time I had been wasting with certain people. I never before considered that they were taking my existence from me, but they were."

At that point in my life, I had many friends who were in the habit of dropping by to visit or telephoning me at whim. Because I am a writer and my office is in my house, they assumed I was available for talk or advice on any subject. But after that conversation with Stirling and Bruce, I realized that instead of spending time with them I had been wasting it.

I bought a large "Do Not Disturb" sign that I hung outside my office door and I installed a telephone-answering machine. To my surprise, my work output almost doubled. I had taken a step toward controlling my use of time.

———————————————⊙———————————————

**Life unfolds on a great sheet called Time,
and once finished it is gone forever.**
—CHINESE ADAGE

———————————————⊙———————————————

ACTIVE
INACTIVITY

*B*ronislaw Kaper, who introduced me to the martial arts more than two decades ago, introduced me to another interesting notion—consciously doing nothing. Bronny is courtly, elegant, and a gentleman in the European style. Born in Poland and educated in Warsaw and Berlin, he was a junior sabre champion by the age of eighteen and is still considered one of the best sabre-men on the West Coast, even though he is now in his late sixties.

One day I telephoned him to see whether he was available for lunch. "Sorry," said Bronny, "but this is my day for doing nothing."

I protested, "But lunch is not doing anything but eating."

Bronny laughed. "If I made a date for lunch with you, dear boy, I must do something and today I do nothing."

"Explain, please," I said.

"In our lives today, we don't leave room for empty spots, for doing nothing. This concept of *doing nothing,* which has nothing to do with just not doing something, is also an activity and an exercise.

43

"Compare doing nothing to a pause in music. A pause is not a lack of music, it is an integral part of the composition. If a conductor does not hold a pause to its full value, it is like cutting into the flesh. As Claude Debussy has said, 'Music is the space between the notes.' The masters of good phrasing, like good martial artists, are men who pay as much attention to pause and silence (nonaction) as to action."

Bronny seemed to be saying that meaningful pause allowed one to take stock of where one was. The next time I saw Bruce Lee, I told him of my conversation with Bronny.

Bruce laughed and said, "He's right, you know. That pause in the middle of action is one of my secrets, too. Many martial artists attack with the force of a storm without observing the effect of their attack on their opponent. When I attack, I always try to pause—stop action—to study my opponent and his reactions before going into action again. I include pause and silence along with activity, thus allowing myself time to sense my own internal processes as well as my opponent's."

Years later, long after Bruce had gone to make films in Hong Kong, I finally understood how important this "stop action" was to his art. Most martial artists use a set pattern of techniques repeatedly. But Bruce was never locked into a routine. He was, in a sense, constantly conducting an environmental impact report on his own activity—pausing to assess, adjust, and correct according to the demands of the situation. He never allowed his opponent to dictate his actions. Instead, he forced his opponent to react to him, pausing frequently to regroup and reform his approach.

Recently I found a way to fit this abstract idea of "stop action" into my life. For some time I had allowed my work schedule to pattern my life. Then one day I was overwhelmed by the pressure. I realized that there was a parallel with my experiences on the mat when engaged in a bout with an overpowering opponent. During such a bout, I often heeded Bruce's words and paused to regroup and then attempted to take the initiative. Why wouldn't this method work with my present problem?

Despite all the pressures, I decided to take a day off, a pause during which I planned to do nothing, and study the situation. The pause worked wonders for me. I assessed my predicament, settled on a future course of behavior, and decided that I would take the initiative in determining my own life schedule. I had discovered that doing nothing can sometimes be more important than doing something.

The mind should be nowhere in particular.
—TAKUAN

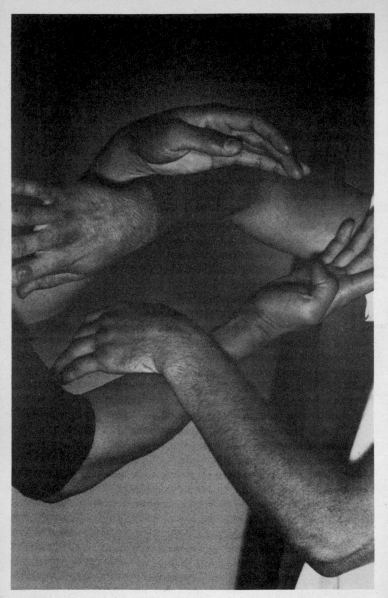

INACTIVE
ACTIVITY

Jim Lau, my sifu in wing-chun, is twenty-eight years old and cast from the same mold as Bruce Lee. As a youth, Lau studied wing-chun in Hong Kong under Bruce's master, the legendary Yip Man. Lau is of medium height and slight, with arms and legs of tempered steel but as flexible as willow wands. He can stand nose to nose with an opponent and still kick him in the jaw!

As a first-time visitor to Jim Lau's wing-chun academy in a converted store in Los Angeles, I was surprised to discover all the students wearing street clothing. Lau himself was wearing a red Mickey Mouse T-shirt and blue sweat pants. When we were introduced, I bowed to him as is customary when one meets a martial artist of higher rank. He ignored my bow, shook hands, and insisted I call him Jim.

That air of informality is typical of wing-chun, also called "Chinese pugilism," which is now one of the most popular martial arts styles in Hong Kong and Europe and is quickly gaining popularity in America because of its simplicity and realistic approach to fighting. Wing-chun has no system of rank, no colored belts to designate novice from instructor. When a student has reached a certain level of proficiency, the sifu may give him a small medallion or personal token of esteem.

Unlike Bruce, who was dedicated to becoming a film star, Jim Lau's primary ambition is to introduce his art to a growing number of devoted followers, most of whom have come to him experienced in other martial arts. Despite Jim's casual teaching style, he feels a great responsibility for the progress and welfare of each student.

One day recently we were practicing "sticking hands," an exercise in which your hands seem to stick to those of your opponent's—thus its name. Through this training, wing-chun students learn to interpret the silent messages telegraphed by their partner's hands. The way in which a hand retreats can signal a shift of body weight, a change in posture, and/or the probable direction of the next punch. It can give a clue to whether the next blow will be an uppercut, a roundhouse swing, or a straight thrust. Losing contact with your partner's hand allows it to strike you. Pushing against his hand overextends you, and you can easily be knocked off balance.

In this exercise, both partners try to interpret the other's signals while concealing his own. The technique teaches you to ward off an oncoming attack and still remain centered and in control, neither overreacting nor underreacting. The result is often a stalemate.

The exercise frustrated me because Jim was able to read my intentions through the sensitivity of his touch on my hands, much as a mentalist reads minds. I frequently became impatient and attempted to land a blow; but Jim sensed my intention each time, countered the move even before I made it, and always caught me off balance. Finally he stepped back and held up his hand, signalling the end of my lesson. I walked with him to his car.

"You must learn to allow patience and stillness to take over from anxiety and frantic activity for the sake of doing something," he said. "Between martial artists of

the first rank, there is room for only one mistake. Before an exchange of blows, several minutes may be spent in controlled patience and planning while each man respectfully observes his opponent, studying his position or stance, watching, getting ideas, and charging his energy. When one man thinks he is going to attack, his opponent may quickly change his stance. If he has overreacted, his opponent makes a note of it. This is a weakness which he will later attempt to use to his advantage.

"A good player recognizes these moves for what they are: a process of sounding out and experimentation. The good player is patient. He is observant, controlling his patience, and organizing his composure. When he sees an opportunity he explodes."

Some time later I watched a "crossing of hands," or match, between two martial arts masters. I had gone expecting to see a magnificent display of flashing acrobats and whirling limbs. Instead I saw two men in fighting stance study each other warily for several minutes. Unlike boxing, there were no feints, no tentative jabs. For the most part, the masters were still as statues. Suddenly, one of them burst into movement so quickly that I was unable to grasp what had happened, although I did see his opponent hurtle backward. The match was over and the two masters bowed to each other.

I told Jim about this event at my next lesson. "Now you have seen the power of controlled patience on the mat," he said. "The same thing applies to problems in life. When a problem arises, don't fight with it or try to deny it. Accept and acknowledge it. Be patient in seeking a solution or opening, and then fully commit yourself to the resolution you think advisable."

You and your opponent are one.
There is a coexisting relationship between
you. You coexist with your opponent
and become his complement, absorbing his attack
and using his force to overcome him.
—BRUCE LEE

EXTEND
YOUR
KI

I came to aikido, "the gentle art," late in my martial arts studies. I was aware of aikido, of course, and was interested in learning it someday, but I was heavily involved in karate and thought I would wait. Then on a visit to London some years ago, I noticed a poster advertising an aikido lecture and decided to attend.

The lecture took place in a store converted into a small dojo within the shadow of the London post-office tower. The practice hall was packed with spectators sitting cross-legged on a mat watching the master, a young Japanese wearing a white tunic and black *hek-ama,* or skirt, the aikido costume of a master.

He looked fragile and vulnerable as he faced half-a-dozen burly men who circled him menacingly. As they began to close in on him, the master remained still, calm, and poised, standing in the eye of the hurricane. Suddenly with loud shouts they attacked him in unison. What happened then was magnificent. The master seemed to flow like water into the mass. Swirling between them, his black skirt seemed to surround them. Every time they reached to strike his body, it was not there. As a gyroscope spins faster and faster, its motion appears more calm; so it was with the master as he diverted the energy of his attackers and projected them one by one out of the mélée.

It was over in moments. The master, still calm, his mouth set in a slight smile, turned to the audience and bowed to their applause. He then bowed humbly to the student attackers who, in turn, bowed respectfully to him.

The master's actions looked so effortless that I knew there was something below the surface which could not be readily seen, something unexplained. So there was, he said. It was *ki,* the invisible life force or energy that cannot be seen but that most martial artists, especially aikidoists, train to develop.

As a further demonstration of ki he invited any interested spectator to attempt to lift him off the mat. This seemed relatively simple to me so I volunteered. I got a firm hold around the instructor's midsection and heaved, but I was unable to budge him. Although I outweighed him by at least forty pounds, he seemed rooted to the ground. He then asked me to punch him. Before my fist had traveled half the distance between us, I felt myself politely but firmly guided to the mat. I had never been thrown so quickly nor had I ever felt such gentle strength.

"That is an example of ki," he told me, helping me up.

"And how can I develop it?" I asked.

"Only with practice and a proper mental attitude," he answered enigmatically.

I made a mental note that when I returned to Los Angeles I would investigate aikido further.

I sought out an aikido school and began to study this art which was new to me. I constantly heard ki mentioned, and after one of my early sessions asked an assistant instructor, a slim brunette, to explain it to me.

"No one can really explain it, Joe," she said, "but you can experience it. I am going to stand on the edge of the mat with my arm extended straight from the shoulder while you walk toward me and into my arm."

I did as instructed and walked up to her arm, which halted my progress.

"Fine," she said, "now this time I want you to think forward to an object in front of you, beyond my arm and walk toward it."

Again I followed instructions and walked forward "through" and beyond her arm.

"That time you were projecting your energy forward properly," she said. "Now, extend your arm straight out from the shoulder and rest your hand on my shoulder. Make your arm rigid."

Pressing on the inside of my elbow with her hands, she bent my arm quite easily.

"Now bend your arm slightly at the elbow and relax it while it's on my shoulder. Imagine your arm is a hose with water flowing through it and out your fingers in a stream which you have mentally aimed at infinity."

This time she pulled with both hands on my arm but despite her force and leverage was unable to bend it farther.

"That's an example of ki," she said. "Everyone has it to some extent—even a baby. Have you ever tried to pick up a child or a dog who did not want to be lifted? The child seems heavier when it is not cooperating, but when the child wants to be picked up it is lighter. That's because the mind is truly a source of power, and when mind and body are coordinated, ki manifests itself. With practice you can turn ki on at will."

"And where does this ki come from?" I asked.

"The center for ki is the 'one point' or *tai-ten*," she said, pointing to a spot about an inch and a half below her navel. "This is about where the center of gravity for the human body is. Ki is defined as an energy or inner strength that can be directed from the 'one point' through visualization to places outside the body. It can be combined with gravity to produce dead weight and extreme heaviness within the body, as in the case of the child who does not want to be lifted.

"Aikidoists, as well as most martial artists and Zen practitioners, believe that all of the ki, or energy, of the universe flows through them at this 'one point,' traveling forever in all directions. No matter where you are, you are always the center of the universe. By holding your 'one point' and remaining centered, you feel one with the universe and, at the same time, totally aware of your bodily relationship to the universe."

I shook my head. "That's a bit too esoteric for me."

"Here's another way to look at it," she said. "Think of the belly as a valve which sends water (or ki) through all the extremities. When the valve is open, more water (or energy) is generated through the legs and arms.

"If you imagine all your energy coming into your body at a point in your midsection, running down through your legs and running up through your trunk, through your arms, and up into your head—and then, with your mind, you project this energy through your body in the direction you wish—you can be said to be extending your ki. Ki can be sent in any direction, depending on what you plan to do."

I find this an especially difficult concept to understand. But on rare occasions I have been aware of a spontaneous flow of steady strength (or energy) flooding my entire body without consciously seeking it.

Everyone, including nonmartial artists, is capable of drawing on this super power, or inner strength. For instance, the frail woman who batters down a heavy door because her child is locked in a burning room, the husband who is able to lift a car because his wife's leg is pinned underneath—under normal circumstances, these people would not have been able to achieve such feats of strength. But in an emergency, the mind works swiftly and coordinates its strength with that of the body, a technique the martial artist develops through practice until it becomes mechanical and then spontaneous.

For me, the lesson in this can be reduced to a simple statement: It is sufficient to know that there is such a think as ki, an available inner strength that expands the concept of one's own resources. Merely knowing that ki exists in all of us is, in itself, empowering.

Flow with whatever may happen
and let your mind be free: Stay centered
by accepting whatever you are doing.
This is the ultimate.
—CHUANG-TZU

ZEN
BREATHING

*I*t was bone-chilling cold. Breath turned to mist in front of my eyes, and my thin gi was clammy to the touch. Outside it was still dark; the sun would not rise for half an hour. Inside the dojo there were twenty of us, all wearing gis, kneeling on thin mats, backs erect, facing the instructor.

He was kneeling facing us, a wooden block in each hand resting lightly on his knees. He spoke softly, and although he seemed to be staring into space, I was certain he saw each of us clearly.

"When you breathe you must fill your entire lungs with air," he said. "Most people use only the top portion of their lungs. They do not fill up the bottom part. If you breathe correctly you will use the bottom of the lungs as well as the top, the same way you automatically breathe when asleep.

"Imagine that the air you are breathing is fog, and visualize it coming through your nose and throat into the lower abdomen. Let it circulate there and through your body and your limbs. Visualize it as it travels around the various channels and meridians of your body. When you exhale, see the fog leaving your mouth.

"In the beginning, you may become overly conscious of your breathing and begin to pant as though you were doing heavy exercise. When this happens, just start over again."

The sensei's hands arched gracefully together in front of his face as he struck the blocks together. At the sound of the sharp clack, I inhaled slowly and evenly through the nostrils, mouth closed gently so the abdominal wall was stretched, letting the breath circulate inside my body for about ten seconds until the sound of wood on wood struck again.

There was a gentle whooshing sound as we all breathed out together, exhaling about three-quarters of the air through our mouths. Then the sharp clack penetrated the room, and we inhaled again.

Soon a rhythm was established; the clack, a whispering sound as twenty people inhaled, and then a clack and a sound like a sigh as we exhaled in unison.

For the first few minutes I remained chilled, my body stiff, rebelling at the posture and the hard floor. But as the breathing exercise progressed, I became warm and my body was completely relaxed. By the time the first light of morning illumined the room, I was perspiring heavily and ready to begin the lesson.

The breathing-in and breathing-out exercise is not as simple as it seems. In the beginning, I seemed to be the only one in class who could not stay with the rhythm. I was either taking in too much air, or letting out too little or too much, and ending up breathless within a matter of moments and having to start again.

In time I realized the wisdom of the sensei's image: By trying to visualize the breath as fog, other thoughts were kept from my mind, and with total concentration on breathing, I soon relaxed. My mind was calm but alert, and my physical being serene. I was ready to go on the mat because I could flow easily in any direction, like water. And if I were thrown I would land gently like an infant dropped on a mattress.

I remember how fascinated I was by the fact that even such a simple thing as breathing was subject to being relearned and mastered, as part of martial arts training. I had no awareness then that there would come a day when the controlled-breathing technique I had learned would save my life.

Some time later, in October 1972, I was on holiday with my wife, Elke, in Europe. One lovely summer morning we were driving through the wine country of France when I felt an agonizing pain in my abdomen, compounded by a splitting headache. Soon my entire body ached with excruciating pain. Within an hour, I was writhing on the seat and intermittently lapsing into unconsciousness. My teeth chattered and my body convulsed with coughing attacks. I had to ask Elke (who, fortunately, was driving) for a tissue so that I could wipe my lips, because I was too weak to pluck one from the box. Elke quickly took the tissue from me, glanced at it, and threw it out the window. I later learned that it was covered with blood.

Elke began driving at a furious pace, taking unpaved roads and driving on sidewalks to gain time. She knew of a university clinic in Freiburg just across the border in Germany, and we could be there within minutes. I drifted in and out of consciousness as if in a dream.

By the time we arrived in Freiburg, pain filled every joint in my body. When Elke found a doctor he came to the car and immediately called for a stretcher. I have only vague memories now of being wheeled into an examining room and given some tests.

I have a clear memory, though, of the doctors telling Elke in German that I was not only vomiting blood but also voiding it. I then heard him ask her if there were any next of kin to be notified, and I knew I must be dying. I panicked. My heart started palpitating, and each heartbeat shook my body. The doctor who was attending me thought I was having a heart attack and had a fibrillator prepared to regulate my heartbeat.

At that moment I thought, "This is absurd. I am sick enough without adding a heart attack to my problems." With my breathing labored, my heart palpitating, and my body tense, I began forcing myself to regulate my breathing by taking deep belly-breaths (the stomach goes out during inhalation), holding for one, two, or three seconds, and then forcefully expelling all the air. I repeated the process until I settled into a relaxed belly-breathing that required my concentration, inhaling through my nose for four counts and exhaling through my mouth for four breaths. This technique, which I had been taught as a prelude to aikido, is an aspect of Zen practice that makes one oblivious to external impressions. The more I concentrated on my breathing, the more immune I became to the fear that I was dying. Within a few minutes I was in control of myself and my body again.

Before the fibrillator reached my bedside, my heartbeat was normal. *"Unglaublich,"* the doctor said in German. "Incredible."

I lapsed into unconsciousness again and was brought to the clinic's intensive care unit where I remained for five days. Twice during that time my fever reached 106°, and the doctors told Elke they had lost me. Of those moments, I recall only floating in a cocoon of warmth down a narrow tunnel where I would be free of pain. I could hear Elke's voice from a distance pleading with me not to die.

Each time this happened I began to regulate my breathing. Three weeks later I was discharged from the hospital. I had survived a case of Weill's disease, a rare virus which is usually fatal. (I was the first case in Germany in over forty years.) According to the Institute for Tropical Disease, I had contracted it from some foul water in Spain.

Had this incident befallen me a few years earlier, I

would certainly have died because the Zen breathing technique was not yet known to me. Since then I have found the technique especially useful in stressful or anxiety-provoking situations when my breathing becomes irregular and fear distorts orderly thought processes, which tend to immobilize both my body and mind.

Before certain business meetings or personal confrontations, I try to put myself into a relaxed state by controlling my breathing; this relaxes and refreshes me as well as calming my mind. Controlled breathing restores calm, confidence, and strength.

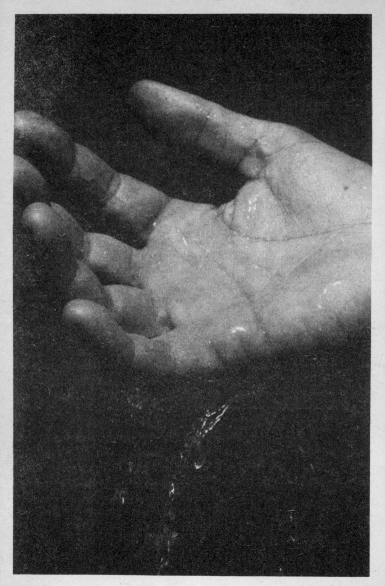

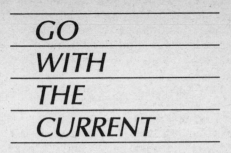

GO
WITH
THE
CURRENT

.

My partner and I were practicing *shomen-ate,* the first movement of the *randori no kata* in aikido class. The exercise called for me as the defender to avoid a straight punch to the face by moving inside the attacking arm and projecting the attacker backward by placing my hand on his chin and moving in with my body.

I closed with my partner several times but was unable to budge him. Finally, in some desperation I applied physical force, and he toppled to the mat. Then I felt a light tap on the shoulder and turned around to find the assistant instructor frowning at me.

"You met the force of his attack head on," she said reprovingly. "Because you are strong you got away with it, but all you did was stop his force, not his intention to attack.

"When someone hits you, he is extending his ki toward you and it starts to flow when he thinks he will hit you—even before his body moves. His action is directed by his mind. You don't need to deal with his body at all if you can redirect his mind and the flow of his ki. That's the secret; lead his mind away from you and the body will follow."

"And how can I lead his mind away from me?" I asked.

"By not upsetting the flow of his ki or making him aware of your intention. You don't pull, push, or hit. You merely touch his body softly and gently and guide it where you wish. That way his mind is not upset and his body will follow.

"The principle underlying aikido," she continued, "is to yield to an oncoming force in such a way that it is unable to harm you and, at the same time, change its direction by pushing it from behind instead of attempting to resist it from the front. The aikidoist never goes against his opponent's strength. Rather, he redirects the strength away from him.

"The principle of avoiding conflict and never opposing an aggressor's strength head-on is the essence of aikido. We apply the same principle to problems that arise in life. The skilled aikidoist is as elusive as the truth of Zen; he makes himself into a koan—a puzzle which slips away the more one tries to solve it. He is like water in that he falls through the fingers of those who try to clutch him. Water does not hesitate before it yields, for the moment the fingers begin to close it moves away, not of its own strength, but by using the pressure applied to it. It is for this reason, perhaps, that one of the symbols for aikido is water."

Shortly after the lesson I had an opportunity to test some of the aikido principles the instructor had given me. During a business meeting I realized a confrontation with an associate was imminent. Determined to skirt it if possible, I avoided reacting to his initial attack to prevent a head-on clash. As the dispute continued I admitted that his argument had some merit. At the same time I tried to deflect his anger in another direction. By allowing my "opponent" an opportunity to expend his energy and anger and by not responding or giving anything back, the confrontation was avoided. In time, he shrugged and walked away.

Softness triumphs over hardness,
feebleness over strength. What is more
malleable is always superior over that which is
immoveable. This is the principle of
controlling things by going along with them,
of mastery through adaptation.
—LAO-TZU

ANGER
WITHOUT
ACTION

*W*ing-chun workouts are often conducted at close range, and I soon became accustomed to feeling blasts of wind as hands and fists whirred dangerously close to my eyes and face. Occasionally a partner would accidentally make contact, and then I would feel a surge of anger.

One day after a workout, Jim Lau called me aside. "When you get hit you stiffen, and I sense anger and a desire to strike back," he said.

I was ashamed. He had read my reaction all too well. "I know I shouldn't get angry, but I can't help it," I said.

Jim smiled. "It's not bad to have aggressive or hostile thoughts and feelings towards others. When you acknowledge these feelings you no longer have to pretend to be that which you are not. You can learn to accept these moods. What is bad, however, is letting them dictate your nature. When you unleash your aggression or hostility on another person, it inspires aggression and hostility in return. The result then is conflict, which all true martial artists try to avoid. Anger doesn't demand action. When you act in anger, you lose self-control."

Jim looked at me thoughtfully. Then he spoke again. "How can you expect to control someone else if you cannot control yourself? Think about that as an essential quality of martial arts."

The following weekend I went to New York for a business meeting. After a night flight I arrived at my hotel at 7 A.M., only to find that my room would not be ready for four hours. I was tired and had been looking forward to being able to get some rest before my appointments.

I asked to see the manager, all the while working myself into a rage, rehearsing in my mind what I would say if he or she were unable to provide the room quickly.

When the manager arrived I was fuming. I spoke in anger. My antagonism provoked anger from her, and soon we were in a heated argument. I had forgotten Jim Lau's words and had inspired a head-to-head conflict.

Later, when I was cooler, I apologized to the manager for my bad manners. "You really took me by surprise," she said. "I intended to do what I could for you, but when you came on so strong I forgot my good intentions and decided not to go out of my way to help you."

I saw again the practical application of martial arts to life. The experience taught me a lesson I will not soon forget. Rarely does anger avail. When you lose your temper, you lose yourself—on the mat as well as in life.

Control your emotion or it will control you.
—CHINESE ADAGE

The angry man will defeat himself in battle
as well as in life.
—SAMURAI MAXIM

RECOGNIZE
A TRUE
THREAT

*B*efore I started to study martial arts, I was easily intimidated by false images of strength—aggressive browbeaters, uncompromising people, musclemen, arrogant intellectuals, haughty waiters, persistent salesmen, disdainful automobile dealers. In a confrontation with any such person I usually reacted in an extreme manner. I either quickly retreated from the field, feeling completely inadequate, embarrassed, and angry with myself, or I flashed back with anger, putting myself in direct conflict.

My reaction on the mat against an intimidating, aggressive opponent was usually the same, and so were the symptoms. I became tense, flushed, and tended to overreact.

One day Bruce Lee took me out onto the center of the driveway at my home. He had me stand still and extend one leg as far as it would go. Then he had me pivot slowly around while he drew a chalk circle around me, whose radius was the length of my extended leg.

Bruce then stood some distance from me on the edge of the circle and made some feinting and aggressive moves. I stiffened, awaiting his attack.

"You're tense," he said, "but why? From this distance, I can't possibly cause you any harm."

He then closed the distance slightly, until his feet had penetrated the circumference of my circle. Again, I started to tense and again Bruce chided me. "I'm still not close enough to do you any harm, so why don't you relax?"

Suddenly, Bruce stepped fully into my circle. Instinctively, I retreated. "Good," he said, "You've moved your circle back so I am no threat to you. Now, suppose I stand at the edge of your circle. Am I a real threat to you?"

I shook my head. "Not really. But, suppose I am physically threatened within my circle?"

"When your opponent is inside your circle and you cannot or will not retreat any farther, you must fight. But until then, you should maintain your control and your distance."

As my martial arts ability increased, so did my confidence. I was able to stand calmly back and let an opponent wear himself out with feints or attempts at intimidation because I was confident that, if necessary, I could defeat him.

I soon had an opportunity to translate this attitude to my business life. One day in a meeting I was faced with an aggressive person accustomed to winning arguments by putting subordinates on the defensive. I quickly realized that since his attempts at intimidation were not a real threat to me—after all, I did not work for him—there was no need for me to react aggressively, and I was confident that my work was well done. He was trying to provoke me with words only, so if I could keep him at the edge of my mental circle he would soon exhaust all the hostile energy he could muster without having received any further stimulation from me.

The would-be intimidator thrives on evoking a response from his intended victim. When there is none, he quickly wears out, which is what happened. The man finally shrugged his shoulders and gave up. There had been no real conflict between us, yet he had lost the match.

Here is Master Han's advice for warding off intimidating people and situations. "I never make an instant decision, even when it is between friends," he said. "The proper system is to think twice more. Patience is part of it. To avoid being intimidated—think more and react less."

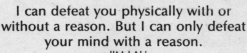

I can defeat you physically with or
without a reason. But I can only defeat
your mind with a reason.
—JIM LAU

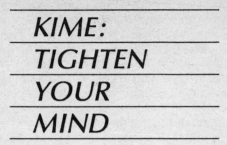

KIME:
TIGHTEN
YOUR
MIND

*I*t was probably a ridiculous sight: two middle-aged men wearing headgear and boxing gloves pummelling each other in the driveway of a suburban home. But Stirling Silliphant and I were trying to put into practice some of the jeet-kune-do techniques Bruce Lee had taught us.

I was concerned with demonstrating to Bruce how much I had learned that my focus was scattered. I had been trying to anticipate Stirling's moves rather than respond to them; I was concerned with my footwork instead of letting my training lead me naturally to the right position. I was concerned with everything but the immediate objective—to get in and score.

"All right, that's enough," shouted Bruce, who had been acting as umpire-coach. "You move like elephants, kick like draft-horses, and telegraph your punches like Samuel Morse."

Bruce then turned his attention to me. "Joe," he said, "you are thinking about blocking Stirling's punch rather than intercepting his fist and landing one yourself. I don't know where your mind is, but it's not where it belongs. You should be concerned with keeping so much pressure on Stirling that you mess up his footwork, balance, and ability to move. And look at how exhausted you are, yet you accomplished nothing."

This was only the beginning of a devastating critique that ended with, "How many times have I told you both to concentrate all the energy of the body and mind on one specific target or goal at a time. The secret of *kime* (tightening the mind) is to exclude all extraneous thoughts, thoughts that are not concerned with achieving your immediate goal."

Later, Bruce chatted alone with me for a few minutes. "A good martial artist puts his mind on one thing at a time," he said. "He takes each thing as it comes, finishes with it, and passes on to the next. Like a Zen master, he is not concerned with the past or the future, only with what he is doing at that moment. Because his mind is tight, he is calm and able to maintain strength in reserve. And then there will be room for only one thought, which will fill his entire being as water fills a pitcher. You wasted an enormous amount of energy because you did not localize and focus your mind. Always remember: in life as well as on the mat an unfocused or 'loose' mind wastes energy."

"And if I can't empty my mind of other thoughts, then what?"

Bruce laughed. "Then your mind isn't tight," he answered somewhat circularly.

It has taken me a long time to master kime and I still have a long way to go, but I have found that when my mind is tight, my mental and physical energies are joined and focused. On those days when I have worked with total concentration, I have accomplished more and ended the day less tired than on days when I was easily distracted.

You may train for a long, long time,
but if you merely move your hands and feet
and jump up and down like a puppet,
learning karate is not very different from
learning to dance. You will never have reached
the heart of the matter; you will have
failed to grasp the quintessence of karate-do.
—GICHIN FUNAKOSHI

MUSHIN: LET YOUR MIND FLOW

After a brisk workout in the sun, Bruce Lee and I were having a glass of juice in the garden. He was relaxed, and it seemed a good time to ask him a question that had been on my mind for some time. "What would happen in a real battle in which you were forced to fight for your life? How would you respond and what would you do?"

Bruce became serious, put his glass down on the table, and cupped his fingers under his chin—a sign that meant he was considering my question carefully.

"I've thought about that often," he said finally. "If it was a real fight, I'm certain I would hurt my assailant badly, perhaps kill him. If that happened and I was forced to stand trial, I would plead that I had no responsibility for my action. I had responded to his attack without conscious awareness. 'It' killed him, not me."

"What do you mean by 'it'?" I asked.

" 'It' is when you act with unconscious awareness, you just act. Like when you throw a ball to me and, without thought, my hands go up and catch it. Or when a child or animal runs in front of your car, you automatically apply the brakes. When you throw a punch at me, I intercept and hit you back, but without thought. 'It' just happens."

He noticed I was still puzzled, and he laughed. "This is something else for that book you're always planning to write," he said. " 'It' is the state of mine the Japanese refer to as *mushin*, which literally means 'no-mind.' According to the Zen masters, mushin is operating when

the actor is separate from the act and no thoughts interfere with action because the unconscious act is the most
free and uninhibited. When mushin functions, the mind
moves from one activity to another, flowing like a
stream of water and filling every space."

"And how does one attain this state of no-
mindedness?" I asked.

"Only through practice and more practice, until you
can do something without conscious effort. Then your
reaction becomes automatic."

"I'm going into my office for a tape recorder," I said.

"You do that," said Bruce. "Meanwhile I'll get a book
for you from my car."

When I returned to the garden, Bruce had a worn volume in front of him. It was a book by the great Zen master and swordsman Takuan, who was one of the first to apply Zen to the psychology of swordsmanship. Bruce opened the book and read aloud:

"The mind must always be in the state of 'flowing,' for when it stops anywhere that means the flow is interrupted and it is this interruption that is injurious to the well-being of the mind. In the case of the swordsman, it means death.

"When the swordsman stands against his opponent, he is not to think of the opponent, nor of himself, nor of his enemy's sword movements. He just stands there with his sword which, forgetful of all technique, is ready only to follow the dictates of the unconscious. The man has effaced himself as the wielder of the sword. When he strikes, it is not the man but the sword in the hand of the unconscious that strikes."

Bruce paused. "Now do you understand what I mean by 'it'?"

I understood the concept intellectually, but it was years before I understood it in my bones. After many months of practicing a particular wing-chun movement with Jim Lau—the movement called *bong-sao,* an elbow-in-the-air block—there came a day when the elbow suddenly flew up without conscious thought.

"Very good," said Jim. "You didn't even think about it, but your *bong-sao* was perfect."

In time, many more of my movements just happened correctly. Mushin was beginning to function. I realized that I was letting my mind flow instead of confining it to thoughts about what I was doing. My responses were becoming instinctive and immediate—the result of long hours of practice and confidence in the teacher and in the teachings.

Soon after I thought I had learned mushin I went on the mat for another wing-chun match, full of confidence, certain that I was, though not undefeatable, at least formidable. "It" was ready to work for me. From the beginning things went badly: My opponent scored with relative ease while I was waiting for "it" to happen, which it never did. And the more I thought about "it", the more flustered I became.

When I told Jim Lau about my defeat, he laughed. "You thought you had learned a lesson and then, as we all do, you forgot the point of the lesson," he said. "You blocked. When you think of showing off your skill or defeating an opponent, your self-consciousness will interfere with the performance and you will make mistakes. There must be the absence of the feeling that you are doing it. Self-consciousness must be subordinated to concentration. Your mind must move freely and respond to each situation immediately so there is no self involved.

"For example, if you are fearful your mind will freeze, motion will be stopped and you will be defeated. If your mind is fixed on victory or defeating your opponent, you will be unable to function automatically. You must allow your mind to float freely. The instant you become conscious of trying for harmony and make an effort to achieve it, that very thought interrupts the flow and the mind blocks.

"Now you have the key to the ancient Zen riddle, 'When you seek it, you cannot find it.'

"Your mind will invariably stop if you direct your attention to the thought of attack or defense. These thoughts create an opening called a *suki*, an interval, and they give your opponent an advantage because you can't respond fast enough to counter his move."

"And how can I unblock the blockage?" I asked.

"The worst thing to do is to try to block the blocking. The best thing to do is just accept it when it occurs. You will find it usually dissolves itself."

"Is there no other way to unblock my thoughts?"

"Yes," said Jim. "Keep at your training so that you act unconsciously instead of intellectually."

"We've come full circle to mushin," I said.

"We have," he said. "Have you ever noticed how simply a good professional athlete performs? Training and practice take over from conscious striving, and he just does it. I'm sure Jimmy Connors doesn't think of hitting the tennis ball any more than Arnold Palmer is concerned with addressing a golf ball. They just lay into it. Skiers sense the terrain they are on and when they are required to make an adjustment, it's automatic, without thought—mushin."

TRY SOFTER

A young boy traveled across Japan to the school of a famous martial artist. When he arrived at the dojo he was given an audience by the sensei.

"What do you wish from me?" the master asked.

"I wish to be your student and become the finest karateka in the land," the boy replied. "How long must I study?"

"Ten years at least," the master answered.

"Ten years is a long time," said the boy. "What if I studied twice as hard as all your other students?"

"Twenty years," replied the master.

"Twenty years! What if I practice day and night with all my effort?"

"Thirty years," was the master's reply.

"How is it that each time I say I will work harder, you tell me that it will take longer?" the boy asked.

"The answer is clear. When one eye is fixed upon your destination, there is only one eye left with which to find the Way."

—ANONYMOUS

INSTINCTIVE ACTION

Some martial artists achieve a state of awareness suggestive of a sixth sense; this is the total involvement in environment for which Zen practitioners aim. It produces a calmness and detachment even in the face of threatening situations, when fear or anger might seem the natural response.

Because of his training, an expert martial artist reacts not in a personal way but almost like natural law. Lightning strikes so thunder booms; the wind blows and the tree bends; the attack comes and the response follows. "It" happens.

In the classic Japanese film *The Seven Samurai,* some unemployed samurai are given a trial of swordsmanship. Inside the doorway of a building through which everyone entering must pass, a village leader has hidden a young man. As soon as a samurai tries to step over the threshold, the young man is to strike him suddenly with a stick and see how the warrior responds.

The first swordsman receives the stick with full force and fails the test. The second man dodges the blow, strikes the young man in return, and is disqualified for reacting in anger. The third samurai senses the presence of an enemy inside, stops at the entrance, and tells the man hiding inside the doorway not to try such a trick on a fully seasoned warrior. He proves to have the sixth sense that the village elders seek.

To know and to act are one and the same.
—SAMURAI MAXIM

In order to achieve victory you
must place yourself in your opponent's skin.
If you don't understand yourself, you
will lose one hundred percent of the time.
If you understand yourself, you will
win fifty percent of the time. If you understand
yourself and your opponent, you will win
one hundred percent of the time.
—TSUTOMU OSHIMA

Technical knowledge is not enough.
One must transcend techniques so that the
art becomes an artless art, growing
out of the unconscious.
—DAISETSU SUZUKI

UN-THINKING
PAIN

Martial artists, or *karateka,* are frequently injured in the course of practice. For this reason they have had to develop effective ways of coping with pain. Since most martial artists are not Zen masters but practical men who practice Zen they rarely philosophize about what they have learned, though they frequently share their experiences with each other.

One afternoon in the spring of 1975, I visited the dojang of Yong Tae Lee, a seventh-degree master of tae-kwon-do. Lee had agreed to a match with boxer Mike Quarry to be held at the Houston Astrodome that summer, and I went with Pat Strong to Lee's studio to watch him work out.

We found him alone in a corner of the dojang pounding his bare fist on a *makawara* board—a thick wooden post bolted to the wall and covered with rice straw secured by thin ropes. His concentration was so complete that he was unaware he had visitors. Blood was trickling from Lee's knuckles onto the board, but he kept smashing it powerfully and rhythmically over and over for several minutes before looking up. Then he saw us and came across the mat.

Although neither tall nor heavy, Lee seemed mammoth. He gave the appearance of having been poured into a tattered black gi. Every inch of the fabric was strained by powerful muscles. His feet resembled blocks of oak but he moved effortlessly, as though he were being tugged toward us by a rope attached to his center of gravity. I remember thinking that the mere sight of him on a mat would give any opponent cause for fear. But his face was serene and his eyes and mouth smiling as he bowed and then shook hands with me in the traditional manner—left hand lightly touching my right wrist.

I noticed that the knuckles of his right hand were almost raw pulp and asked him if his hand hurt. Lee said it had not hurt until just now when he thought about it.

"But it must have hurt during the workout," I said.

Lee shook his head "no" and told us the following story. "My master in Korea was eighty-eight years old when he got a severe infection in his nose and sinuses. The doctors said he had to have immediate surgery. When they tried to give him an anesthetic to kill the pain, he refused. The doctors were afraid to operate on him without administering the drug, but my master was determined.

"Finally, the doctors agreed but asked me to stand by. My master closed his eyes and relaxed as the doctor inserted his scalpel. The surgery lasted for two hours, and my master never moved or winced with pain. The expression on his face never once changed.

"When the operation was over, he opened his eyes and got off the table. The reason my master did not show his pain is that he put his mind elsewhere."

"How is that possible?" I asked.

"Regulate your breathing, fix your eyes and mind on something else—perhaps a rock or a spot on the floor or ceiling. Concentrate on that object, savor it, taste it, give it color and smell the dimension. Let it absorb all your thoughts and concentration and the pain will diminish. When I was striking the makawara board as you came in, my mind was on my home in Korea. Though I was standing in my dojang, I was seeing the mountains I knew as a youngster and the children I played with, hearing their laughter and my mother's voice. I was unaware of the pain in my hand.

"As you see, my mind was elsewhere. Without mind there cannot be pain. Once you can conquer pain, your whole attitude about the conquest of other things less harsh than pain is enhanced."

Some days after the visit with Lee, I went to the dentist for some routine dental work. The doctor suggested an injection of Novocain to kill the pain. Remembering what Lee had told me, I decided to test his technique and have the work done without anesthetic.

I asked for a minute or two in which to prepare myself, and I started to regulate my breathing, fixing my eyes and mind entirely on a spot on the ceiling, as Lee had explained. Within a few minutes the dentist was finished and I realized I had not even been aware that he had been at work.

Recently another experience gave support to Lee's technique. One day while working out I pulled a muscle in my back, and the pain was so great I collapsed on the floor as though I had been shot. I found myself crying from the pain. I began to analyze the pain itself, to savor it, to attempt to assign it a taste, a smell, and to visualize it in color. Although the pain still existed, it quickly seemed less intense because my brain was investigating it.

The mind's power of concentration is stronger than pain when the martial artist has learned to use the Zen technique of "mind over matter."

EFFORTLESS
EFFORT

A good martial artist should be able to go from any position or stance and strike his opponent without telegraphing his intention. This technique, sometimes called "sparking," can be achieved only in the absence of previous conscious thought—instead, the thought and the action must be simultaneous.

During one of my wing-chun sessions with Jim Lau, Jim stood facing me with a baseball mitt in his hand and asked me to hit it before he could move his hand. Each time I threw a punch, however, he sensed my intention and moved the mitt. Although I had begun the exercise with a relaxed body and mind, I was soon tense and straining, frustrated by the fact that he was able to anticipate my actions. Even when he finally held the glove almost still, I was unable to land a punch.

"Relax," he said. "Stop straining. The less effort, the faster and more powerful you will be."

We continued the exercise until I was exhausted and therefore totally relaxed. Finally, not caring whether I hit the target or not, I saw an opportunity and snapped my fist; my hand landed on the mitt with a satisfying thud.

"Perfect," Jim shouted. "At last you sparked properly. And do you know why? Your mind and body were relaxed. You stopped caring whether you hit or not. It is the caring or desire which stands in the way of effortless effort."

I backed off and faced him again, determined to repeat the achievement. But I failed.

"You're trying too hard," Jim said patiently. "Stop caring."

"But what good is it to me to be able to hit when I *don't* care about it? When I *want* to, I can't!"

"You must stop caring about doing it and just do it—effortlessly and naturally as snow falls from a tree or water bubbles up from a spring. After you have practiced something for a long time, it becomes second nature. Don't be concerned with making contact with the mitt, just throw your hand out without conscious effort. Let it happen."

It was many weeks later before I duplicated my original feat and, again, it happened when I had almost given up and no longer cared.

"Aha!" shouted Jim. "That time you didn't care, and it happened. At last you are beginning to understand the secret. But if I had told it to you, you would never have understood. The knowledge had to come from inside."

"I know it but I don't know it," I said truthfully.

"Then I will put it into words for you," he replied. "Relaxation and concentration go hand-in-hand. But too much concentration defeats itself. If you are truly relaxed, and allow the body and the unconscious to do their share, instead of working the conscious mind overtime, concentration can become effortless effort."

"That's all well and good for you to say," I answered. "But when a fist is about to bury itself in my midriff or nose it's not easy to be uncaring."

Jim's comment to that was, "Don't care so much."

Later that week when I was playing tennis I fixed on a phenomenon I had noticed before: Very often when a serve was long or a trifle out I returned it perfectly. I

realized that when the serve was out of the court there was no need for me to make a good shot; so I casually hit the ball without thought or care and, generally, made a first-rate return. Now I knew what Jim meant: What stands in the way of effortless effort is caring, or a conscious attempt to do well.

During my next few tennis lessons I made up my mind to stop straining and just accept each lesson as a game; it was unimportant whether I was good or not. When I stopped straining, it happened. I had made the break-through.

I then transferred the same principle to my work. Although faced with what seemed to be an impossible schedule, I said to myself, "To hell with it. I'll just do it." My concentration was focused, but I was relaxed physically and mentally. I did what had to be done in less time and with less effort than I would have thought possible. By caring less and not worrying about the job at hand, I was free to get on with it. The effort was effortless.

The mind of a perfect man is like
a mirror. It grasps nothing. It expects
nothing. It reflects but does not
hold. Therefore, the perfect man can
act without effort.
—CHUANG-TZU

The less effort, the faster and more
powerful you will be.
—BRUCE LEE

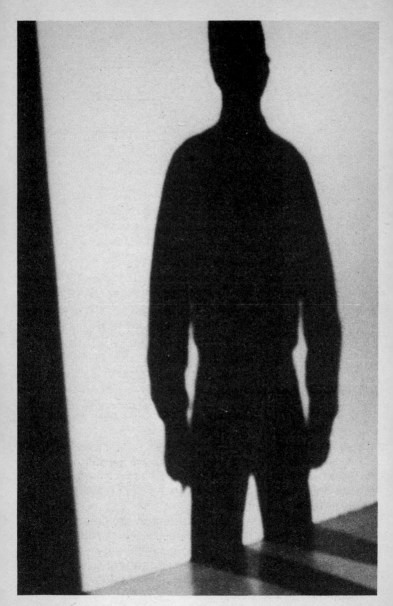

MAKE
A FRIEND
OF FEAR

*I*t was only a bare foot, but I was unable to keep it from landing someplace on my body. My breath was labored and my arms and legs felt like lead weights. Every time I moved, that foot seemed to find an opportunity to land with sufficient force to knock the breath out of me. If I were not careful, it might dislocate or even fracture my jaw. My opponent had hands, too, but it was his feet I feared.

When the match was over, I was completely exhausted. My mouth was dry, and I was perspiring profusely. Master Han, who had been watching the kumite, called to me. I went to him, bowed, and stood silently awaiting his comment.

"You cannot run away from fear in the dojang," he said. "In fact, it's a perfect place in which to learn to face fear. Most of the time we generate our own fears, and this is especially true when we confront an unfamiliar situation that shatters confidence. And this is what happened to you today."

Suddenly, without warning, his foot swept up from the floor toward my head. Without thinking my hands flew into a guard position and I took a huge step backwards and out of range.

"Don't move!" he commanded. "I'm not going to hit you."

Again his foot snapped up, stopping a whisker's breadth from the right side of my jaw, then speedily reappearing at the left. I heard the snapping sound of his gi trousers as his foot grazed the tip of my nose. I was trembling, but I had not moved.

"Good," he said. "Remain still and composed, secure in the fact that you are in no danger."

I did as ordered. For the next few moments I heard only the snapping of the gi as his foot whipped around my body, always stopping short of making direct contact.

"You must develop the confidence to handle fear," he said. "I will have a student practice kicking at you every day that you come in, with instructions that he is never to make contact. Until your fear of being kicked becomes familiar and you develop confidence, stand still and do not react. In time you will no longer be afraid. This I promise you."

He bowed to me, signifying the end of the lesson. Later, when I had changed into street clothes and was about to leave, Master Han beckoned for me to enter his office.

"I have a story to tell you," he said. "When I was a boy growing up in Korea I was terrified of the ferocious tigers that still live there. During the early stages of my martial arts training my master, who knew of my fear, told me that while meditating I should visualize myself battling a tiger. In the beginning, the tiger always defeated me. Then I began to go to the zoo in Seoul and study the tigers there, familiarizing myself with their habits and movements.

"In time I realized that although the tiger was fearsome indeed, he did have weaknesses: He did not have complete mobility of his jaws, and he relied strongly on his hind legs for tearing at his opponent. I began to work out strategies for my imaginary bouts with the tiger, to find ways of exploiting his weaknesses. Soon I occasionally won a skirmish, and my fear of tigers began to disappear."

Master Han smiled and gestured toward the walls of his office. "Now you see the walls here are covered with pictures of tigers. When I am alone, I study one of the pictures and imagine myself in conflict with the animal. Sometimes I win and sometimes I lose. But I am no longer afraid because they are familiar to me. In the heat of combat I am calm, which is as it should be because I have discovered that fear is shadow, not substance."

It took me many weeks of constantly facing the kicks of Master Han's students before I realized that when I was afraid, I was usually frightening myself, and that my own fears were only one aspect of a situation which could just as well be viewed without trepidation. When I accepted the fact that I was frightening myself, I became less frightened. My lack of self-confidence caused the problem.

Having overcome some of my fears, I know now that it is better to face a fearful situation than to ignore it, to accept the fact that it's all right to be fearful. For example, I once put off an emotional confrontation that I feared. When I realized that the confrontation was inevitable, I began to visualize the forms it could take. I began to face and analyze my fears. What was the worst that could be said, and how might I react?

By visualizing the possibilities over a period of time, I reduced my fears to their proper proportions. I was finally ready for the encounter. Of course, it turned out to be far less difficult than I had originally feared.

CONFIDENT
SEEING

*O*ne of the first lessons one learns in the dojo is that the mind is a powerful factor in everything you do, including those exercises that seem to require a maximum of physical strength. For instance, the first time I confronted a brick that I had to break with the edge of my hand, I was certain it would be my hand and not the brick that would break. I relayed my fear to Pat Strong, my long-time instructor and friend.

"I want you to make several passes at the brick," he said. "Think to yourself, 'this is how I will break it.' Then visualize the underside of the brick. Don't consider the top of the brick, just think about the bottom. When you feel ready, clear your mind of all thoughts except the image of your hand passing through the brick."

He then set the brick to be broken atop two other bricks, forming a small arch. I kneeled in front of the bricks and brought my hand down slowly, stopping at the outer surface of the brick but visualizing my hand coming through to the underside. "Now!" shouted Pat. To my surprise I sliced the brick neatly in half, scarcely aware that I had done it.

I soon learned that almost all successful athletes use

this system of visualization. At that time I was writing a book about tennis with Billie Jean King, and I asked her why she so rarely double-faulted under pressure in a match. "Before the second serve I visualize it going in," she said. "I never permit myself to think for even a moment about the possibility of a double-fault."

But what if negative thoughts do enter the mind? During one of my last workouts with Bruce Lee, my mind was on a letter I had received from a publisher asking me to rewrite a number of chapters of a book on which I had already spent a great deal of time. I was depressed, convinced that the book was not publishable. Bruce instantly sensed that my concentration was elsewhere and asked if this were so. I admitted my preoccupation and told him what was bothering me.

"The mind is like a fertile garden," Bruce said. "It will grow anything you wish to plant—beautiful flowers or weeds. And so it is with successful, healthy thoughts or with negative ones that will, like weeds, strangle and crowd the others. *Do not allow negative thoughts to enter your mind for they are the weeds that strangle confidence."*

"That sounds just fine," I said, "but the thoughts are there. How do I get rid of them?"

"I'll give you my secret for ridding my mind of negative thoughts," Bruce said. "When such a thought enters my mind, I visualize it as being written on a piece of paper. Then I visualize myself wadding the paper up into a tight ball. Then I mentally light it on fire and visualize it burning to a crisp. The negative thought is destroyed, never to enter my mind again."

"Beautiful!" I said. "But how can I develop the confidence to do the job?"

"By visualizing success rather than failure, by believing 'I can do it' rather than 'I can't.' Negative thoughts are overpowering only if you encourage them and allow yourself to be overpowered by them."

I realized then that negative thoughts were indeed overpowering me, although I rationally knew I could do the job. I had never thought of visualizing the problem solved or the work done, as Bruce suggested. Nor had I ever "thought through" the problem, as Pat Strong had taught me to do with the brick. But this time when I started the rewrite, I kept the thought of success uppermost in my mind and quickly finished.

This technique of visualization is used by martial artists in many situations. For example, karate instructor Sam Brodsky recently planned a demonstration for his students in which he intended to break nine one-inch slabs of concrete with one punch of his fist.

The concrete was stacked on the floor in front of him and Brodsky took a half-kneeling position. He made two false passes at the brick, then inhaled deeply. With an ear-splitting "Kiai!" (exhalation of breath) he smashed his fist onto the slabs. All but the last two shattered. After the applause, I noticed Brodsky's face turn white and he turned the class over to an assistant.

I found him in the dressing room examining his hand with dismay. It was clearly injured. Although he was almost certainly in pain, he gave no sign of it as he left, saying he thought he had better see his doctor.

Later I learned that he had pulverized many of the small bones in the knuckles of his right hand. The doctors called the damage a "displaced fracture" and decided to operate. After the operation his hand was put together with wires, and Brodsky was told it would take fifteen to eighteen weeks for any kind of healing process to begin. The doctors said it would probably be a year before he regained even partial use of the hand.

Brodsky, who had studied martial arts in Korea and Japan, believes that the key to healing lies in the mind. On the night he came home from the hospital with his hand in a cast, he lay in bed with his eyes shut, imagining that his hand was a building site.

Here is his story: "As I lay in bed, I imagined a whistle going off and I visualized a horde of little men with mortar and cement and welding tools climbing down inside the cast going to work on reconstructing my hand. The men had different colored work clothes and hard hats, even slogans on their T-shirts. I concentrated so hard on the way they were dressed and their tools and equipment that I forgot the pain. Then sleep came.

"In the morning I woke up imagining that I heard the whistle going off. It was as though the little men had worked a full night shift putting together the bones in my hand.

"Every night for three-and-a-half weeks before I went to sleep I heard that whistle going off and 'saw' those little men at work on my hand. They had pulleys hooked up to the bone with braces and couplings.

"Two weeks later when I went back to see the doctor, he took my hand out of the cast and said the healing process was 'amazing,' but that my knuckles were frozen together. I would have a stiff hand. He put my hand in a sling and sent me home.

"Each night from then on, before I went to sleep, I imagined the same men at work on my hand. But this time their equipment had changed. Now they were working with files, oil, graphite, and materials that lubricate and make things smooth. They began filing and sanding my knuckles. When I went back to the doctor again seven weeks later, he said it was 'a miracle.' The healing process, which he had estimated would take a year, had required only ten weeks."

Six months after his hand had healed, Brodsky successfully completed the demonstration before his students.

Last winter I used Brodsky's technique of visualizing the healing process to clear up a severe bronchial congestion. Every morning and evening for three successive days, I carefully visualized a snow-blower moving through my bronchial tubes, clearing out the congestion and opening up the passages. I practiced seeing myself getting healthy, and very soon I was.

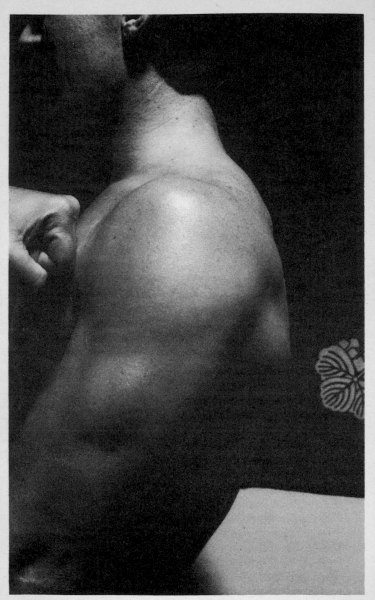

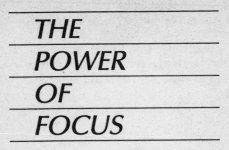

THE POWER OF FOCUS

Bruce Lee was only 5 feet 8 inches tall and weighed less than 150 pounds, yet the amount of power he was able to generate was incredible. One of his favorite demonstrations of power was his "one-inch punch"— holding his hand only an inch away from the chest of a man far larger and heavier, Bruce was able to either knock the man down or propel him backward.

One day while Bruce was training me in my backyard, a friend who had heard about Bruce dropped by to watch the session. My friend was a black belt in judo as well as a weight lifter. He watched us quietly for a few minutes. Then, because the young master was not formidable in appearance, he decided to *put Bruce to the test.* He told Bruce that although his lightning-fast movements were impressive, he wondered how much power they had.

"Enough to do the job," Bruce said quietly.

My friend was stubbornly determined to challenge Bruce, and when the session was over he brought up the question of power again.

Bruce asked my friend to take a position about five feet from the swimming pool.

"Brace yourself," said Bruce, as he placed his hand, fingers outstretched, on my friend's brawny chest. "I am only going to close my hand into a fist and I will knock you over."

"No way," said my friend, who nevertheless braced himself.

Bruce suddenly closed his fingers into a fist—a movement of perhaps one-quarter of an inch—and my friend flew backward into the pool.

As he climbed out dripping wet, my friend merely asked meekly if he could go into the bathroom and towel off.

I followed him into the house and found him sitting on the edge of the tub, fighting hard to catch his breath, and examining his chest. "I feel as though I've been hit with a hammer," he said. "I wouldn't have believed it."

Later I asked Bruce how he had done it.

"I relaxed until the moment I brought every muscle of my body into play, and then concentrated all the force in my fist," he said. "To generate great power you must first totally relax and gather your strength, and then concentrate your mind and all your strength on hitting your target."

Again, I decided to try to apply the principle of focused concentration to my tennis game. During a warm-up, when I was normally a bit tense, I made a conscious effort to relax and gather all my strength until the moment I made contact with the ball. Then I concentrated only on stroking the ball properly, keeping my mind on the area of the court where I wanted the ball to land. The ball left my racket with tremendous speed and went exactly where I intended it to go. It was a far better shot than I have ever before made. And whenever I remember Bruce's demonstration of focused power, I have been able to duplicate it.

A Zen master out for a walk with one of his students pointed out a fox chasing a rabbit. "According to an ancient fable, the rabbit will get away from the fox," the master said.

"Not so," replied the student. "The fox is faster."

"But the rabbit will elude him," insisted the master.

"Why are you so certain?" asked the student.

"Because the fox is running for his dinner and the rabbit is running for his life," answered the master.

MULTIPLE
OPTIONS

Mas Oyama is a Korean who teaches karate in Tokyo. Although only forty-four years old, Oyama is a master among masters, considered by many to be the greatest living martial artist. His exploits are legendary. To develop his discipline, endurance, and body he spent a year and a half living alone in the desolate mountains of Japan, doing 2,000 push-ups a day and pounding his fists against trees until they were bloody. To develop concentration he sat under an ice-cold waterfall and meditated on Zen koans (questions that cannot be resolved by rational thought), creating a state of intellectual tension conducive to attaining enlightenment.

Oyama can drive the edge of his hand through a dozen roofing tiles as easily as a woodsman can chop a bough with an axe. I have seen film in which he faced alone the onslaught of a charging bull and brought the huge animal to the ground with two blows. The first blow sliced a horn in half; the second hammered the animal squarely on the head and stunned it.

He is a big, Buddhalike man—solid, permanent, and at one with himself and his environment. The landscape of his face is flat, tranquil, and bland, with just the hint of a smile around the edges of the mouth. It is his eyes which rivet you: intelligent, calm, clear, and aware. He gives the impression of seeing and comprehending everything. He is usually silent, sitting quietly, hands resting on his thighs. Everyone who comes into his presence is calmed by his serenity.

When asked about the source of his tranquility, Oyama's answer is oblique, as are many of the answers given by Zen masters: "Karate is not a game. It is not a sport. It is not even a system of self-defense. Karate is half physical exercise and half spiritual. The karateist who has given the necessary years of exercise and meditation is a tranquil person. He is unafraid. He can be calm in a burning building."

After having spent many years with martial artists, I think I understand the underlying meaning of Oyama's words. Such serenity can only be achieved by fully extending yourself in what you do, knowing that you have done everything you are capable of doing. Because Oyama has pushed himself to the outer limits of his mental and physical abilities, nothing can unnerve or worry him.

When Oyama performs karate, one has the sense that he is wrapped in an impenetrable cocoon of his own experience, excellence, and self-knowledge. He is never nervous about his performance, since he is always functioning within an area he has already fully explored.

He epitomizes the Zen master in combination with the master of the martial arts. Because of his detached calm, he is capable of making a rational decision from his many possible options even in the face of life-threatening danger.

Oyama, like many other masters who have dedicated their lives to martial arts, has learned that there are multiple ways of responding to an attack on the mat just as there are multiple courses of action available in any life situation. Because Oyama is calm and sure of himself and his abilities, he can respond with force as easily as he can respond gently.

My own experiences on the mat have taught me that there are certain things I can do something about and others about which I can do nothing. I have learned to consider the alternatives with a kind of detached calm, and having made a rational decision, to follow through with it.

Even in the face of an earthquake a martial artist would probably maintain his calm and his sense of proportion. At the first rumble he would say to himself, "I'm in an earthquake. What is the best thing to do? Should I get under a doorway? Should I run outside? Should I remain where I am?" Were he to decide to move, he would do so calmly because his decision was based on rational thought. Whatever his decision, he would react to the facts of the situation and not to the fantasy or the threat.

The American karate master, Ed Parker, likens this state of tranquility to having "a mind like still water" *(miso no koro)*.

How does one achieve "a mind like still water?" One learns to go with the flow of life, the current of existence. When an untoward event occurs in your life, react to it without haste or passion. Realize that in almost every instance you probably have more alternatives than you think you have. Hold still a moment before acting or reacting and consider the alternatives. Then, having decided upon a course of action, proceed calmly.

MARTIAL
ARTS
WITHOUT
ZEN

Not long ago I observed a dispute between two martial artists of the first rank. One of them was an instructor with his own dojo, the other had been his best friend—until he decided to open up his own school. In the process he took with him several students from his friend's dojo.

As an intimate of both men I was astonished to discover their irrational hostility toward one another. There was talk of vendettas between the schools, personal confrontations, recriminations, and vows of enmity. They displayed all the behavior one might expect of misbehaved children, indicating to me that it is possible to be a martial arts master without mastering the spirit of Zen.

This may seem at odds with much that I have written about in this book, but the simple truth is that it is possible to master the physical techniques of the martial arts without understanding or absorbing the spiritual and philosophical basis of the arts. On the other hand, it is also possible to apply the spiritual precepts of Zen in the martial arts without involving oneself in the arts.

I believe one can learn much about Zen from any activity one is engaged in by remaining aware of one's inner reactions. The key is a constant exercise of awareness, vigilance of the mind, and relaxation of the body. Applying the principles of Zen frees an individual from concern, tension, and anxiety about winning or losing.

Since I began studying the martial arts many years ago, I have noticed both small and large changes in my attitudes and my actions. For example, all of my other sports activities have improved. I am a better tennis player because I am able to hit the ball without thought, freeing my body and allowing me to relax physically as well as mentally. I run better because I am not concerned with running a certain distance or for an established length of time.

My attitude toward my work has also changed. Years ago I thought too much about what I had to do, labored too long over it, put off difficult chores, waited for the mood to be right or the creative juices to flow. Now I just do it without conscious effort. It flows because the work and I are one, and not in conflict with each other.

The study of Zen in the martial arts has also helped me alter my personal life. I feel my life calmer, richer, and fuller. I now have more patience, more tolerance of others, and more self-confidence. I feel myself to be a better father, husband, and friend. I have lost much of the edginess and combativeness that arose from my insecurity. Of course, I would still rather not lose a game, a bid for work, or an argument. But when I do, I can now lose more graciously, accepting defeat as part of the learning process.

THE WAY OF LIFE

A man is born gentle and weak.
At his death he is hard and stiff.
Green plants are tender and filled with
 sap.
At their death they are withered and dry.
Therefore the stiff and unbending is the
 disciple of death.
The gentle and yielding is the disciple of
 life.
Thus an army without flexibility never wins
 a battle.
A tree that is unbending is easily broken.
The hard and the strong will fall.
The soft and weak will overcome.
—LAO-TZU

KARATE
WITHOUT
WEAPONS

*T*here have been numerous books about karate written by the masters. In my view, the best of all these books was written by the greatest of all the masters, Gichin Funakoshi. At nearly ninety years of age he wrote his autobiography, *Karate Do: My Way of Life.* In telling of his own famous teachers, not only of their mastery of technique but also of their behavior in critical situations, Funakoshi reveals the true spirit of karate.

One of my favorite stories in his book concerns one of his teachers, Master Matsumura. The story begins some decades ago in Naha, Japan, in the small shop of an engraver who was also the local karate champion. The engraver was a giant of a man, with bulging muscles straining the short sleeves of his kimono. Just past forty years of age, he was in the prime of his manhood.

One day Matsumura came into the engraver's shop. Although not as formidable in appearance as the engraver, Matsumura, who was in his early thirties, was also an imposing man—tall, with piercing black eyes. But his voice was soft as he described a design he wanted engraved on the brass bowl of his pipe.

The engraver looked up at his visitor. "I beg your pardon, sir," he said. "But aren't you Matsumura, the karate teacher?"

"Yes," said Matsumura. "What of it?"

"You are said to be the finest karate instructor in the land. You even teach the head of the clan, don't you?"

"I did," said Matsumura with bitterness. "But no longer. To tell the truth, I am fed up with karate."

"I don't understand," said the engraver. "Everyone knows you're the best sensei alive. If you are no longer teaching the head of the clan, then who is?" Noticing the look of dejection on Matsumura's face, the engraver added, "Something dreadful must have happened."

"You are right," said Matsumura. "The head of the clan was an indifferent student with crude technique who is accustomed to winning matches because of his rank, not his skill. One day, to teach him a needed lesson, I pointed out his weaknesses and dared him to attack me with all his strength. He opened with a double kick *(nidangeri)*—a bad first move to use on an expert—and I sent him sprawling in a heap six yards away.

"When he finally regained his footing, he ordered me to leave his sight and not return until I was sent for. It would have been better for me had I never attempted to teach karate to him in the first place. In fact, I'd have been better off had I never learned karate myself."

"Nonsense," said the engraver. "In any event, since you are no longer teaching him, why don't you teach me?"

"No," said Matsumura. "As I told you, I've given up teaching and, in any case, why would a man as expert as you want to take lessons from me?"

"Frankly, I'm curious to see how you teach," said the engraver.

"I don't teach karate anymore," thundered Matsumura, irritated by the engraver's presumption that the former teacher of the head of the clan might become an engraver's teacher.

At this outburst the engraver's attitude changed. "Then, if you refuse to teach me, will you also refuse to grant me a match?"

Matsumura was incredulous. "You want a match—with me?"

"Exactly," replied the engraver. "There are no class distinctions in a match, and since you no longer teach the head of the clan you don't need his permission to meet me." The engraver's voice and eyes now had a touch of insolence as he said, "And I can assure you that I'll take better care of myself than he did."

"Don't you think you are going too far?" asked Matsumura. "It's not a question of being hurt, it's a matter of life or death. Are you so set upon dying?"

"I'm quite willing to die," snapped the engraver.

"In that case I will be happy to oblige you," said Matsumura. "But first let me remind you of the old saying, If two tigers fight, one is bound to be hurt and the other to die."

When Matsumura saw his words had no effect on the engraver, he said, "I leave the time and place of our encounter up to you."

And so an appointment was made for five o'clock the following morning in the graveyard behind Tama Palace. At the appointed hour the men met. Dispensing with formalities, they faced each other from a distance of many yards. The engraver made the first move. He closed the gap by about half, thrust out his left fist in a *gedan* position, and cocked his right fist at his right hip, ready to attack.

Matsumura quietly faced him in a natural position *(shizen tai)* with his chin resting at his left shoulder. It was a posture that seemed to offer no hope of defense, and the engraver prepared to continue his attack. At that moment, Matsumura opened his eyes wide and looked deep into the eyes of his opponent. Although Matsumura had not moved a muscle, the engraver fell back, repelled by a force that felt like a bolt of lightning.

Sweat beaded the engraver's brow and poured from under his arms. His heart began pounding. Feeling faint, he sat down on a nearby rock. Matsumura casually did the same.

After a moment Matsumura shouted, "Come on, the sun is rising. Let's get on with it."

The two men rose and Matsumura assumed the same stance. The engraver, again determined to attack, advanced toward his opponent and once more was repelled by a force he later swore came only from Matsumura's eyes.

Now aware that the match was lost but determined to die like a man, the engraver gave a mighty *Kiai!* (a roar) which had terrorized lesser opponents. But Matsumura stood unmoved and once again the dismayed engraver retreated.

"Why don't you attack?" Matsumura asked.

"I don't understand," the engraver replied. "I've never lost a match before but I would rather be dead than lose face. I warn you, I'm going to attack in *sutemi*," (meaning he would fight to the finish).

"Good," said Matsumura, smiling. "I await your pleasure."

Suddenly the engraver launched his attack with all the skill he could command, but at that very moment there came from Matsumura's throat a shout which echoed across the cemetery and rebounded from the distant hills. As the lightning from Matsumura's eyes had earlier paralyzed the engraver, so now did the dreadful *Kiai!* freeze him in motion.

"I give up," the engraver cried. "I was a fool to challenge you. There's just no comparison between my skill and yours."

"Not so," replied Matsumura gently. "You have great fighting spirit and, I suspect, much skill. If we had actually crossed hands, I might well have been defeated."

"You flatter me," said the engraver. "The truth is, I felt completely helpless when I looked at you, and I lost whatever fighting spirit I had."

"Perhaps," said Matsumura quietly. "But that was because of the difference between us. You were determined to win and I was just as determined to die if I lost.

"Listen," he added, "When I came into your shop yesterday, I was unhappy about being reprimanded by the head of the clan. When you challenged me, I was worried about that too, but once we decided on a match, all my worries vanished. I realized that I had been obsessed with relatively minor matters—with refinements of technique, with the skills of teaching, with flattering the head of the clan. I had been preoccupied with retaining my position.

"Today I am a wiser man than I was yesterday. I'm a human being and a human being is a vulnerable creature, who cannot possibly be perfect. After he dies, he returns to the elements—to the earth, to water, to fire, to wind, to air. Matter is void. All is vanity. We are like blades of grass or trees of the forest, creations of the universe, of the spirit of the universe, and the spirit of the universe has neither life nor death. Vanity is the only obstacle to life."

With that statement Matsumura became silent. The engraver was quiet, too, pondering the invaluable lesson in karate he had received. He had been defeated by a master without a blow being struck.

As for Matsumura, he was soon reappointed to his old position as personal instructor to the head of the clan.

WINNING
BY
LOSING

When I first started to study martial arts, I had a recurrent daydream: My wife and I were crossing a dark street and were accosted by several thugs, or hoodlums. As the leader of the group stepped forward, I quickly and efficiently dispatched him with appropriate blows and fearsome sounds. In variations of this fantasy, the others of the group also attacked, and I quickly took care of them or they ran away in fear. This would result, of course, in my being a hero in my wife's eyes.

Twenty-five years later, when I had some expertise in the martial arts, a real-life situation took place, whose outcome was totally unlike my imagined scenario. I had just dropped my wife off at Los Angeles International Airport. In my haste to get home, I turned my car down a one-way lane in the parking lot, causing an oncoming car to screech to a halt. The driver shouted abuse at me. I apologized, but he kept up the tirade and blocked my exit. He then got out of his car and came to my window, continuing the harangue.

Again I repeated my apology, but he said he intended to teach me a lesson. I scrambled across the passenger seat and got out the side door to put my car between us.

When he came around the car I was waiting for him, arms at my side, hands open. I had already decided not to do anything unless he entered my "circle." He paused about five feet away and studied me.

"I told you I'm sorry," I said.

"I'm going to rip your tongue out of your mouth and stuff it down your throat," he said.

"Now what would you gain by that?" I asked quietly. "I'm almost twice your age and obviously it's no contest."

He started to edge forward. I shifted my body minutely so that my right foot was slightly forward and my weight centered. I crossed my hands over my chest so that the fingers of my right hand lightly touched my chin. I was staring at him in such a way that no single feature of his body was the point of focus, but I was completely aware of his entire body. I had taken a classic "ready" position from which I could move instantly. My mind was calm, open and relaxed, and I was confident of my ability to handle whatever happened.

"I had to jam on my brakes to avoid hitting you," he said a trifle less aggressively.

"It was my fault," I agreed.

"Yeah, well, okay," he said, and walked back to his car.

Although I stood confident and ready to respond to an attack, it was unnecessary. By apologizing for what was indeed my fault, I had defused his hostility. And by not acting aggressively, I had removed the necessity for him to prove anything by attacking me. I had "won by losing."

Ed Parker says, "The only reason men fight is because they are insecure; one man needs to prove that he is better or stronger than another. The man who is secure within himself has no need to prove anything with force, so he can walk away from a fight with dignity and pride. He is the true martial artist—a man so strong inside that he has no need to demonstrate his power.

"The point of achieving proficiency in any martial art is to be able to walk away from a fight rather than to win it. But you will walk with shoulders erect, pride in your bearing, knowing inside what the outcome of the battle would have been had you wished to precipitate it. And this attitude of confidence will be communicated to your antagonist, who will realize that he narrowly escaped defeat."

The Chinese word for this kind of confidence is *sai,* which can also be defined as "presence." It is a byproduct of self-confidence and is instantly recognizable in any situation. Martial artists who are certain of their ability have it when confronted with certain situations, just as any person who is expert in his field projects it.

To be confident, however, does not mean to be foolhardy. On a recent television show I was asked what I would do if someone stuck a knife in my ribs and wanted my wallet. My answer was immediate. "I'd make change." As Jim Lau says, "There are times when you should fight, and there are times when you should split." I know of no martial artists who would risk their lives to save their wallets.

One day it was announced by Master Joshu that the young monk Kyogen had reached an enlightened state. Much impressed by this news, several of his peers went to speak with him.

"We have heard that you are enlightened. Is this true?" his fellow students inquired.

"It is," Kyogen answered.

"Tell us," said a friend, "how do you feel?"

"As miserable as ever," replied the enlightened Kyogen.

—ANONYMOUS

To win one hundred victories in one hundred battles is not the highest skill. To subdue the enemy without fighting is the highest skill.

—SUN-TZU

ABOUT THE AUTHOR

Joe Hyams began his involvement in the martial arts in 1952 as one of Ed Parker's first students in kenpo-karate. He has studied jeet-kune-do with Bruce Lee in addition to eight other martial arts disciplines. A black belt in karate since 1969, Joe still practices wing-chun. His other hobbies have included fencing, flying, and race-car driving.

Joe Hyams began his writing career as a U.S. Army Combat Correspondent in the South Pacific during World War II. In 1951 he joined the *New York Herald Tribune* and was soon sent to Hollywood as the West Coast Bureau Chief. Within a few months he became one of that paper's most widely syndicated columnists, with more than 3,000 news stories to his credit, and for a decade he was the most highly paid magazine writer in the world, his byline appearing in almost every major magazine. He has also written sixteen books, ranging from his autobiography, *Mislaid in Hollywood,* to biography, including *Bogie,* the bestselling story of Humphrey Bogart. He has written three books on tennis and has two books currently being filmed. He is also the author of numerous screenplays and two novels: *The Pool* and *The Last Award.*

The author lives in Beverly Hills, California, with his wife, actress Elke Sommer, and five dogs.

ABOUT THE PHOTOGRAPHERS

Kenneth McGowan's photographs have been exhibited at the Museum of Modern Art in New York and in solo photo shows at the Leo Castelli Gallery in New York and the Green Collections in Tokyo. He has had his photographs published internationally in *Zoom Magazine* (Paris), *Camera Mainichi* (Tokyo), *Foto* (Stockholm), and *Art Forum* (USA).

Doug Coder's photographs have been exhibited in group shows in Los Angeles at the Cirrus Gallery, the Frankfort Gallery, and the galleries of California State University at Long Beach and of Chapman College.

This is the first time Ken and Doug have collaborated on the photography for a book.

BANTAM NEW AGE BOOKS

Bantam New Age Books are for all those interested in reflecting on life today and life as it may be in the future. This important new imprint features stimulating works in fields from biology and psychology to philosophy and the new physics.

☐	23564	THE PICKPOCKET AND THE SAINT	$4.50
		Sheldon B. Kopp	
☐	14146	SUPERMIND: THE ULTIMATE ENERGY	$3.95
		Barbara B. Brown	
☐	24147	CREATIVE VISUALIZATION Shatki Gawain	$3.95
☐	22511	NEW RULES: SEARCHING FOR SELF-FULFILLMENT	$3.95
		IN A WORLD TURNED UPSIDE DOWN	
		Daniel Yankelovich	
☐	22510	ZEN IN THE MARTIAL ARTS J. Hyams	$2.95
☐	23550	STRESS AND THE ART OF BIOFEEDBACK	$4.50
		Barbara Brown	
☐	23463	THE FIRST THREE MINUTES Steven Weinberg	$3.50
☐	20059	MAGICAL CHILD Joseph Chilton Pearce	$3.95
☐	22786	MIND AND NATURE: A Necessary Unity	$3.95
		Gregory Bateson	
☐	20708	ZEN/MOTORCYCLE MAINTENANCE	$3.95
		Robert Pirsig	
☐	20693	THE WAY OF THE SHAMAN Michael Hamer	$3.95
☐	23100	TO HAVE OR TO BE Fromm	$3.50
☐	23125	FOCUSING Eugene Gendlin	$3.95
☐	23734	LIVES OF A CELL Lewis Thomas	$3.50
☐	14912	KISS SLEEPING BEAUTY GOODBYE	$3.95
		M. Kolbenschlag	

Prices and availability subject to change without notice.

Buy them at your local bookstore or use this handy coupon:

Bantam Books, Inc. Dept NA. 414 East Golf Road, Des Plaines. Ill 60016

Please send me the books I have checked above. I am enclosing $ _____
(please add $1.25 to cover postage and handling). Send check or money order
—no cash or C.O.D.'s please.

Mr/Mrs/Miss_____

Address_____

City_____State/Zip_____

NA—1/84

Please allow four to six weeks for delivery. This offer expires 7/84.